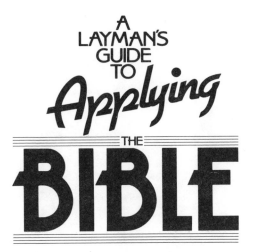

A LAYMAN'S GUIDE TO Applying THE BIBLE

A LAYMAN'S GUIDE TO

Applying

THE

BIBLE

Walter Henrichsen and Gayle Jackson

Lamplighter Books Grand Rapids, Michigan

Zondervan Publishing House

A Layman's Guide to Applying the Bible
Copyright © 1985 by The Zondervan Corporation
Grand Rapids, Michigan

Library of Congress Cataloging in Publication Data

Jackson, Gayle.
    A layman's guide to applying the Bible.

      "Lamplighter."
      1. Bible—Use. 2. Christian life—1960– 3. Word of God (Theology) I.
Henrichsen, Walter A. II. Title.
BS538.3.J33   1985   248.4   85-14524
0-310-37691-2

Edited by Penelope Stokes

Printed in the United States of America

85 86 87 88 89 90 / 10 9 8 7 6 5 4 3 2 1

Contents

Foreword

Gayle Jackson and Walt Henrichsen define obedience as the process of applying God's Word—a process through which God prepares us to live in His presence. They explain valuable principles that can be used to help conform us to the image of Christ.

For many Christians, commitment is out of fashion, and the pursuit of holiness almost casual. Far too many who profess allegiance to our Lord Jesus Christ have become spiritual bystanders, content to observe and interpret and evaluate, but failing to act with a radical, personal application of the truths of God's Word.

Both of these men are my friends. Walt and I worked together for a number of years. Gayle is a committed Christian layman who is well qualified to co-author a book like this. Both practice what they teach in this book.

I commend this *Layman's Guide* with enthusiasm. May it challenge those who read it to a deeper commitment to obeying God's voice in the Scriptures and to find their lives changed for eternity.

> Lorne Sanny
> President
> The Navigators
> Colorado Springs, Colorado

Introduction

Perhaps no generation has faced a greater need for the personal application of biblical truth than our own. We have traditionally looked to our society's institutions to help us in the application process. We expect government to establish legislation that will guard us from sin. We once had laws prohibiting adultery and divorce, and we still have laws against prostitution, pornography, and gambling. Although many of these laws still exist, they are often unenforced.

A divorce is as easy to obtain today as a marriage license. Abortion is as easy as a trip to a clinic. Pornography and illicit sex are available in the living room of the average home through the medium of television. Government seems to have neither the will nor the means to check such abuses.

The church has not fared much better in fighting this onslaught of evil. We are a generation of people who view experience as more valid than propositional truth. We often seem to believe that the Bible is God's Word only to the extent that "it speaks to us," and that the commandments of God are valid only to the degree that we experience their validity. "Thus saith the Lord" has been replaced by subjectivism.

Unfortunately, in our era, the personal application of Scripture is just that—*personal*. If people are not motivated to take seriously the claims of Scripture, they will find virtually no help from society's institutions. More than ever before, the believer is on his or her own in applying the Bible.

This should disturb us but not discourage us. While assistance is helpful, the Bible lays the responsibility for application squarely at each person's feet: "Whoever has my commands and obeys them, he is the one who loves me" (John 14:21).

9

Many passages of Scripture demonstrate personal application. One of the most challenging is Daniel. As he left Jerusalem for captivity in pagan Babylon, he was cut off from all of the institutional props afforded the average Jewish lad. Gone were the temple, the sacrificial system, the priesthood. Daniel was surrounded by a culture riddled with sin and debauchery, yet he survived as a man whom God called "greatly beloved" because he was a willing participant in the application process.

We have designed this book to help in that process. It is not an easy book. It is cerebral rather than visceral. It challenges your thoughts rather than your emotions. Little has been written on personal application, but if individual believers intend to survive the secularization of our culture, they must give careful attention to biblical application.

STRUCTURE OF THE BOOK

The major sections of the book are:
1. *A Perspective on Application*—Chapters 1–3
2. *The Process of Application*—Chapters 4–9
3. *The Principles of Application*—Chapters 10–15

SECTION 1

This section gives a perspective on application—an overview of God's attitude about His Word and its influence in our lives. In this overview, we hope to stimulate an appreciation for the application process.

When God speaks, He expects to be obeyed. Chapter 1 asserts the importance of application, beginning with the recognition of our need for it. From Genesis to Revelation, the importance of applying God's Word is a major Bible theme.

Chapter 2 defines terms. Four words are discussed that relate to the application process: obedience, disobedience, rebellion, and legalism.

Chapter 3 reviews the application process itself, a process that has four phases: recognition, response, results, and rewards. All four must be present before the disciple can experience balanced, continuous growth with God.

SECTION 2

Section 2 addresses the major questions surrounding the process of application. Each chapter's thesis deserves concentrated study, thought, and prayer. This section is encyclopedic and contains individual modules for study; that is, you can take any chapter in section 2 and study it separately. It relates to the whole, but it can stand by itself as well. These chapters are cross-referenced with the application principles found in the third section of the book.

Chapter 4 is about the renewing of our minds, or "filter systems," which is the foundation for change. Frequently, application is thought of as a "do list." However, a more profound aspect of application is the altering of one's filter system, which involves a response described in Romans 12:2: "Do not conform any longer to the pattern of this world, but be transformed by the renewing of your mind." The application process involves bringing our minds into conformity with God's Word rather than bringing God's Word into conformity with our minds.

Chapter 5 explains the risks of this application process. The Bible calls us to do things that our culture has taught us are foolish. We are to forsake all, die to self, serve others, give, become of no reputation. These and similar biblical admonitions are contrary to the way the world thinks, but these risks are necessary to the application process.

Chapter 6 asks, "Who in the world is meeting my needs?" This is a crucial issue in obeying God's Word. Only if we look to God, and God alone, to meet our needs, will we respond properly to the revelation of His Word.

Chapter 7 analyzes our motivation in the application process.

A person is always motivated in the direction of hope. We can tell what a person hopes by what motivates him or her. Just as an Olympic athlete is willing to discipline her body because she hopes for a gold medal, the believer is motivated by God's promises.

Motivation leads to the question of motive—the subject of chapter 8. Many motives are involved in obeying God: a sense of love and gratitude for our great salvation; a respect for God and a belief that what He says is right; and the promise of reward. This chapter comes to grips with a legitimate motive for a life of application.

Finally, chapter 9 discusses the source of application. If our lives are to be marked by a proper response to God's Word, what parts of that Word are we to obey and emulate? Although this chapter may seem technical, it is important in sorting out the numerous examples and commands in the Bible.

When the major questions about applying God's Word are answered, believers can be assured that they are participating in all four phases of that process. Christians must face these pragmatic, gut-level issues if they are going to take seriously the Lordship of Jesus Christ.

SECTION 3

This section contains the twenty-six application principles and, like section 2, is modular in approach. It is divided into six groups:

Foundational Principles of Application—chapter 10
Principles of Personal Responsibility—chapter 11
Principles on Our Perception of God's Word—chapter 12
Principles on the Product of Disobedience—chapter 13
Principles on the Life of Application—chapter 14
Principles on People in the Process—chapter 15

These principles are grouped to facilitate study, and they are cross-referenced with chapters 1 through 9 to aid review. They may be studied in a variety of ways. For instance, each principle can be studied by itself. Or each group can be approached as an independent unit. A third approach is to study them in connection with the chapters in section 2. Although this book can be read by studying any section, chapter, or grouping, it is most effectively studied from beginning to end, with ample time to digest, review, and reflect.

SECTION

A Perspective
on the
Process of Application

1 The Importance of Application

Application is important to God! As we begin reading the Bible, we find that when God speaks, He expects to be obeyed. What happened when God said, "Let there be light"? There was light. Throughout the creation account, when God speaks, He is obeyed. And He is obeyed because He is God, the sovereign of the universe.

God's expectation of obedience is a thread that runs throughout the Scriptures. All men and women of God have recognized the importance of this principle and have responded accordingly.

God used Ezra the priest to bring Israel out of the Babylonian captivity and back to the Promised Land. Ezra's response is typical of all who are pleasing in God's sight: "For Ezra had

17

devoted himself to the study and observance of the Law of the
LORD, and to teaching its decrees and laws in Israel'' (Ezra 7:10).
Ezra had a heart for obedience, and when he discerned what God
wanted, he did it. He is an example of biblical application.

CONVICTIONS, BEHAVIOR, AND FEELINGS

People are more than flesh and bones. They are the product of
their convictions, value systems, and perspectives on life.
Ultimately, people act on what they believe. When a man says
that he is acting contrary to his convictions, he is saying that,
although he knows his action is wrong, his value system can
accommodate it.

The person who desires to follow God finds this pattern:
(1) convictions are shaped by the Scriptures; (2) behavior is the
product of convictions; and (3) feelings are the product of
behavior. In his little book *How Come It's Taking Me So Long to
Get Better?* Lane Adams notes:

> A well-known practicing psychologist told of a trauma that he had
> been going through in his own life because he said, ''I have
> discovered that feelings follow behavior instead of the other way
> around. Since all of my studies in my profession have insisted that
> behavior is a result of one's feelings, it has been a trauma to unlearn
> the one and embrace the other.'' I asked him to explain this startling
> announcement, suggesting that if what he said was right, it would
> revolutionize what was being taught in this realm. Seminaries and
> colleges would have to alter their psychological doctrine to embrace
> such a radical notion. By the time he had offered his rationale to
> support this contention, I was fully convinced.
>
> Out of my own life it makes sense. Misbehavior has always
> produced feelings of guilt in me. Guilt makes me feel lousy. How
> about you? Whenever I resist the temptation to do wrong and my
> behavior is right according to God's will, I inevitably feel good about
> it.[1]

---

[1] Lane Adams, *How Come It's Taking Me So Long to Get Better?* (Wheaton,
Ill.: Tyndale Press, 1981), 80.

The apostle Paul put it this way: "Don't let the world around you squeeze you into its own mold, but let God remold your minds from within, so that you may prove in practice that the plan of God for you is good, meets all his demands and moves toward the goal of true maturity" (Romans 12:2 PHILLIPS).

This verse commands *change*, and that is what application is all about. But change implies the need for standards—standards that, for the Christian, are God's commandments and Christ's character. As we apply God's Word, the Holy Spirit takes it and transforms us into the likeness of Christ. God did not give us the Bible to increase our knowledge, but to change our lives. James defines the challenge succinctly: "Do not merely listen to the word, and so deceive yourselves. Do what it says. Anyone who listens to the word but does not do what it says is like a man who looks at his face in a mirror and, after looking at himself, goes away and immediately forgets what he looks like. But the man who looks intently into the perfect law that gives freedom, and continues to do this, not forgetting what he has heard, but doing it—he will be blessed in what he does" (James 1:22–25).

Our objective in this book is to analyze the components of applying God's Word and to emphasize the importance of this application. Most people, Christian and non-Christian alike, spend the majority of their waking hours being exposed to influences that try to squeeze them into the world's mold. Even Christians who spend time in God's Word often prefer to dissect, analyze, and illustrate the Scriptures rather than trying to apply them.

ASSIMILATING GOD'S WORD

Four ingredients are essential to the assimilation of God's word:

1. *Knowledge.* Many people know a lot about the Bible because its content is available in a multiplicity of forms. People learn about Christ's birth and death through the celebration of

Christmas and Easter, and certain stories are familiar from such films as "Moses" and "The Bible." We learn of David's battle with Goliath and Elijah on Mount Carmel in Sunday school or even through reading Bible comic books.

But we may know a great deal about the Bible and still not understand it. One day my son said, "Dad, I don't want to go to Sunday school anymore. It's a bore." As we talked, he told me that the material was familiar to him—in fact, he knew it better than the teacher did. So as we looked at a passage, I began to ask him why things happened the way they did and what point the author was trying to make. In each case he responded, "I don't know." While knowledge is a good beginning, we must understand the Bible before we can assimilate it.

2. *Understanding.* Understanding is a result of thorough investigation. Each passage should be studied in its broad context and historical setting.

But even understanding, combined with knowledge, is not enough. A person might spend hours studying the book of Job. After each verse is dissected and related to the whole, and after each argument of Job and his friends is thoroughly investigated, the student could have a comprehensive understanding of that book without ever having had a Joblike experience.

3. *Experience.* In addition to knowing and understanding the Word, we must also experience its power. The most important experience of God's Word is conversion. Yet tragically, people sit in church Sunday after Sunday who have never experienced God in a personal way. They might be compared to a man who has courted a woman for years but never married her—it is an unfulfilling relationship.

As important as experience is, however, it is still not the end of the road. One more component is necessary in the assimilation of God's Word.

4. *Application.* Application differs from experience in that a person can experience something but never learn from it. "Some

people,'' a friend of ours once said, ''have ten years' experience. Others have one year's experience repeated ten times.''

Our penal institutions are a tragic example. Many people in the penitentiaries have years of experience, but unfortunately, they have not learned from that experience and have to go through it again and again. Experience does not guarantee application.

In listing these components of assimilating God's Word, we are not suggesting that they must follow in any certain order. For instance, a person may experience something without fully understanding it or make an application without any knowledge of what God says on that particular subject. But of the four aspects of assimilation, application is the most important, the one most heavily emphasized in Scripture.

THE HISTORY OF APPLICATION IN SCRIPTURE

In His relationship with humankind, God expects the same response to His Word as was seen in creation: ''God said, 'Let there be light,' and there was light'' (Genesis 1:3). As far as we can tell, the only creatures who ever dared to disobey God are angels and humans, and of these two groups, only humans have an opportunity for forgiveness, redemption, and reconciliation. The Scriptures seem to indicate that angels, once fallen, have no chance of salvation. By studying the history of mankind's disobedience, we discover not only the importance that God places on obedience but also His infinite love and grace in helping us apply what He knows is best for us.

Adam and Eve. God gave our first parents only one prohibition: ''You must not eat from the tree of the knowledge of good and evil, for when you eat of it you will surely die'' (Genesis 2:17).

Satan challenged this prohibition. His temptation seemed attractive to Adam and Eve as an opportunity to declare their independence—to have their own private Fourth of July. It was an opportunity to gain control of their destiny. God's desire for obedience and man's failure to comply were the preeminent issues in God's relationship to Adam and Eve.

Abraham. When God called Abraham out of Ur of the Chaldeans, He sought to demonstrate to the world what it would be like for a people to look to Him as their ruler. Adam and Eve and their progeny had declared their independence, but through Abraham and his descendants, God would show what being under His authority was like.

From the outset, Abraham's relationship with God was characterized by obedience: "The LORD said to Abram, 'Leave your country, your people and your father's household and go to the land I will show you. I will make you into a great nation and I will bless you; I will make your name great, and you will be a blessing. I will bless those who bless you, and whoever curses you I will curse; and all peoples on earth will be blessed through you.' So Abram left, as the LORD had told him; and Lot went with him. Abram was seventy-five years old when he set out from Haran" (Genesis 12:1–4).

Abraham's readiness to obey God was an important factor in his relationship. His willingness to sacrifice Isaac on Mount Moriah is a supreme illustration of obedience to God. Seventy-five times in the New Testament, more than any other Old Testament figure, Abraham is referred to. Hebrews 11:8–10 is a summary of Abraham's walk with God: "By faith Abraham, when called to go to a place he would later receive as his inheritance, obeyed and went, even though he did not know where he was going. By faith he made his home in the promised land like a stranger in a foreign country; he lived in tents, as did Isaac and Jacob, who were heirs with him of the same promise. For he was looking forward to the city with foundations, whose architect and builder is God."

Moses and Joshua. Moses led the children of Israel out of Egypt, and Joshua led them into the promised land. Among their many similarities, both of these great men of God called the

Jewish nation to obedience. Moses' final words to the nation of Israel were: "This day I call heaven and earth as witnesses against you that I have set before you life and death, blessings and curses. Now choose life, so that you and your children may live and that you may love the LORD your God, listen to his voice, and hold fast to him. For the LORD is your life, and he will give you many years in the land he swore to give to your fathers, Abraham, Isaac and Jacob" (Deuteronomy 30:19–20).

Joshua said essentially the same thing at the end of his life: "But if serving the LORD seems undesirable to you, then choose for yourselves this day whom you will serve, whether the gods your forefathers served beyond the River, or the gods of the Amorites, in whose land you are living. But as for me and my household, we will serve the LORD" (Joshua 24:15).

Moses challenged Israel to choose life or death, while Joshua challenged Israel to choose between false gods and the one true God. In both cases the decision focused on the nation's willingness to obey. The Book of Judges is the record of Israel's response. The theme of this tragic part of Israel's history is "in those days the people did that which was right in their own eyes"—not obedience to God, but obedience to the intuitive observations of life. Obedience to what they *felt* to be right is what motivated them and governed their behavior.

Josiah. Josiah is one of the Old Testament kings during the period of the divided kingdom. After Solomon's death, Rehoboam handled the people foolishly, precipitating a split in the Hebrew nation between the Northern Kingdom of Israel, comprised of ten tribes, and the two tribes of the Southern Kingdom of Judah. Of all the kings in this period, only nine were called "good," and all of these came from the tribe of Judah: David, Asa, Jehoshaphat, Joash, Amaziah, Uzziah, Jothan, Hezekiah, and Josiah. Josiah, the last of the good kings before the Babylonian captivity, lived about 640 B.C., and Hezekiah was his great-grandfather.

Although Hezekiah was considered a good king, in his later years he sired Manasseh, one of the most wicked kings to come out of the line of David. Manasseh had a son, Amon, the father of Josiah. Amon followed in the ways of his father, and God removed them both, bringing Josiah to the throne at the age of eight. At age sixteen he made a decision to follow God's ways: "In the eighth year of his reign, while he was still young, he began to seek the God of his father David. In his twelfth year he began to purge Judah and Jerusalem of high places, Asherah poles, carved idols and cast images" (2 Chronicles 34:3).

Josiah had inherited a kingdom of idolaters. Even during the reign of good King Hezekiah, idols were tolerated, and during the days of Manasseh and Amon, they flourished. The temple was desecrated with idols and male prostitutes, and the country could no longer be distinguished from the heathen nations surrounding it. Josiah had his work cut out for him.

At twenty-seven, Josiah began to purify and restore the temple, during which time the Torah, the first five books of the Old Testament, was found. It had been seventy-three years since the Word of God had been mentioned in the temple. For seventy-three years the nation of Judah was governed without any reference to God's Word.

According to 2 Chronicles 34:14, Hilkiah the priest found the Book of the Law during the cleansing of the temple. Josiah's response to the Word when he had it brought into his presence and read demonstrates his commitment to application:

> Then Shaphan the secretary informed the king, "Hilkiah the priest has given me a book." And Shaphan read from it in the presence of the king.
> When the king heard the words of the Law, he tore his robes. He gave these orders to Hilkiah, Ahikam son of Shaphan, Abdon son of Micah, Shaphan the secretary and Asaiah the king's attendant: "Go and inquire of the LORD for me and for the remnant in Israel and Judah, about what is written in this book that has been found. Great is the LORD's anger that is poured out on us because our fathers have not

kept the word of the LORD; they have not acted in accordance with all
that is written in this book." . . .

The king stood by his pillar and renewed the covenant in the
presence of the LORD—to follow the LORD and keep his commands,
regulations and decrees with all his heart and all his soul, and to obey
the words of the covenant written in this book.

Then he had everyone in Jerusalem and Benjamin pledge themselves to it; and the people of Jerusalem did this in accordance with
the covenant of God, the God of their fathers.

Josiah removed all the detestable idols from all the territory
belonging to the Israelites, and he had all who were present in Israel
serve the LORD their God. As long as he lived, they did not fail to
follow the LORD, the God of their fathers. (2 Chronicles 34:18–21;
31–33)

King Josiah, who sought to be faithful to God before finding
the written Word, was heartbroken to realize how far he and the
nation of Israel had strayed from its requirements. Four
characteristics of Josiah's life were a delight to God: He revered
God's Word; he was teachable; he approached God in humility;
and he was obedient. The narrative gives us God's response to
his attitude: "Because your heart was responsive and you
humbled yourself before God when you heard what he spoke
against this place and its people, and because you humbled
yourself before me and tore your robes and wept in my presence,
I have heard you, declares the LORD. Now, I will gather you to
your fathers, and you will be buried in peace. Your eyes will not
see all the disaster I am going to bring on this place and on those
who live here" (2 Chronicles 34:27–28).

We can learn how to please God from the example of Josiah.
He is a perfect Old Testament illustration of a man who
responded properly to the Word. He did not skirt the issue of sin
or justify himself and his nation; rather, he clearly understood
God's legitimate displeasure with his people and approached
God in humility and with a determination to apply God's truth.
God called him a "good king."

The Hebrews' "Hall of Fame." An overview of the Old

Testament people whom God considers great is recorded in Hebrews 11. Some people refer to this record of the heroes and heroines of the faith as "God's Hall of Fame."

Faith, as demonstrated in Hebrews 11, is a commitment to what God says. There is an important difference between faith and presumption. Faith is acting on what God says; presumption is acting on what we wish God had said, hoping that God will cover for us. Faith is commitment before knowing.

In Hebrews 11, one thing these men and women of God have in common was an active faith. "By faith Abel *offered* . . . ," "by faith Enoch *walked* . . . ," "by faith Noah *built* . . . ," "by faith Abraham *obeyed*." The verbs are all active rather than passive; these men and women acted on what they knew God wanted them to do. A life of obedience is a product of a life of faith.

Jesus. Two complementary themes intertwine themselves throughout the Scriptures and must be clearly understood if one is to make sense of the Bible. The first is salvation. In the words of the apostle Paul, "It is by grace you have been saved, . . . not by works, so that no one can boast" (Ephesians 2:8,9). Salvation is not a product of man's performance; rather, it is a product of God's performance on our behalf in the work of Jesus Christ. Salvation is not through works; it is a gift from God.

Obedience, the second major theme, means applying what we know God wants us to do, that which will delight His heart. We are not saved by our obedience, nor can anyone ever hope to live such an obedient life that he or she does not need the death of Christ. Obedience is the loving response of a soul set free by the saving grace of God. The balance of these two themes can be clearly seen in the ministry of our Lord. Jesus' life and death focused on our salvation. Yet throughout his ministry He constantly emphasized the importance of obedience: "Not everyone who says to me, 'Lord, Lord,' will enter the kingdom of heaven, but only he who does the will of my Father who is in heaven" (Matthew 7:21); "Why do you call me, 'Lord, Lord,' and do not do what I say?" (Luke 6:46); and "Whoever has my commandments and obeys them, he is the one who loves me. He who loves me will be loved by my Father, and I too will love him and show myself to him" (John 14:21).

God's Word and obedience are tied together. The Scriptures communicate God's will to us and become the basis of our application.

Jesus said that a proper relationship with Him implies obedience: "I am the vine; you are the branches. If a man remains in me and I in him, he will bear much fruit; apart from me you can do nothing. . . . If you obey my commands, you will remain in my love, just as I have obeyed my Father's commands and remain in his love" (John 15:5, 10).

Obedience goes hand in hand with "remaining in Christ." Jesus emphasized the importance of the balance even in His relationship with God the Father; "I have obeyed my Father's commands and remain in his love" (v. 10).

WHY IS OBEDIENCE SO IMPORTANT?

Whenever obedience is evaluated in reference to man, it is relative and negotiable. But in reference to God, its importance lies in the fact that He places a premium on it. God considers obedience important because:

1. *It is an indication of our love for Him.* Jesus said, "Whoever has my commands and obeys them, he is the one who loves me" (John 14:21).

2. *Obedience prepares us for our time with Him in eternity.* We go to heaven because of what God did for us in the person of Jesus. What we take with us to heaven is a product of how we have lived on earth, as we will discuss further in the chapter "The Motive of Obedience."

3. *Obedience requires faith, and faith is important to God.* Hebrews 11:6 says, "Without faith it is impossible to please

God.'' Many applications of God's Word do not bring satisfying results. The apostle Paul, for instance, preached the Gospel in obedience to Christ's command, even when the consequences of his obedience were beatings, imprisonment, and rejection. The rewards of obedience may be partially experienced on earth, but often they are received in heaven. Obedience is an act of faith.

4. *Obedience demonstrates our gratitude for what Christ has done for us in His death on the cross.* Paul spends the first portion of many of his letters discussing what God has done for us in the person of Jesus. Ephesians 1–3 and Romans 1–11 are examples. Then Paul explores the implications of the doctrine in the believers' response. Because Christ has done this (first part), therefore we should live like this (second part). In short, the believer's natural response is a life of obedience.

5. *Love for our fellow humans can only be demonstrated through obeying the Scriptures.* ''This is love: that we walk in obedience to his commands'' (2 John 6). This is frequently misunderstood to mean that when people are indwelt by the Holy Spirit, they automatically demonstrate Christlike love. It is not just the indwelling of the Spirit of God, but our *response* to that indwelling, by obeying the Scriptures, that demonstrates the love about which John writes in this verse.

SUMMARY

The entire Bible is the story of God and how people relate to His Word. Scripture indicates the high value God places on an obedient heart. As we see biblical illustrations of people who lived lives of obedience, we conclude that God requires obedience of all believers. Application of God's Word is mandatory for a healthy, growing relationship with Him.

In Psalm 103 God calls us to bless His name. We are to do this by remembering what He has done *and by obeying* His Word. Christ tells us in John 14 that if we love God, we will *obey* His Word! James 1:22–23 tells us that if we are not obeying His

Word, then we are not observing the plight and condition of our lives.

If we embrace this principle, we come face to face with the truth that "whoever has my commands and obeys them, he is the one who loves me." We can no longer face the Throne of Grace and say, "I didn't understand." Once we are challenged with our personal need to apply the Word, we can begin to commit ourselves to it.

At the end of each chapter in Section One and Two, we list principles of application that amplify the chapter's content. The commentary on each principle is given in Section Three. The following principles, therefore, are merely listed for further study. Don't spend time studying them now. Having noted them, plan to return to them after you read through the book.

PRINCIPLES FOR MEDITATION

1.   Application must be focused on pleasing God rather than pleasing others.
12. Knowledge carries with it both a privilege and a responsibility.
24. Our conduct, good or bad, will affect the generations that follow.

QUESTIONS FOR DISCUSSION

1.   In what part of "assimilating God's Word" do you spend most of your time? the least amount of time? How can you design a program that will give you a more balanced approach?
2.   Many people from the Bible were used in this chapter to illustrate the need for application. List as many things that they all have in common as you can.
3.   In what area of your life do you have the most difficulty obeying God? Why?

2 Defining Terms

God places a premium on obedience. When He speaks, He expects to be obeyed. In a biblical sense, the simplest definition for application, therefore, is obeying the Word of God.

Throughout Scripture, however, obedience is discussed in contrast to three other ideas—*disobedience, rebellion,* and *legalism.* Studying these contrasts helps us get a clearer idea of what obedience is.

OBEDIENCE

Obedience is the *process* of applying the Word of God. Culturally, we are goal-oriented, and in discussing obedience we tend to look at the end product. But from God's perspective, the emphasis is always on the process.

31

We can easily detect the moral flaws and imperfections in King David's life. He stole Bathsheba, committed adultery with her, and killed her husband, Uriah. He was often vindictive, and even at the end of his life, his warnings to Solomon included the need to get even with his enemies. We could justifiably challenge whether God was Lord of David's life.

But God's evaluation of David is different: "I have found David son of Jesse a man after my own heart; he will do everything I want him to do" (Acts 13:22). When God's assessment is compared with David's life, we find that God is more process-oriented than product-oriented.

Christians are often uncomfortable when they talk about obedience as a process. End products are clear, crisp, complete, and easy to see and define. We can evaluate and measure them, and compare them with a standard. But a process is nebulous. We can't compare it with an objective standard. Rather, we must look at a person's growth in light of his or her background and future direction.

The process of obedience prepares us for heaven, not for productivity on earth. A man who has difficulty in his marriage because of his past errors may seem unproductive in the cause of Christ. But God is concerned with his growth toward obedience and not his productivity. God's focus is on the process. John 14:21 does not promise better circumstances if we obey, but an increased knowledge of God. *From God's perspective the process prepares us for heaven, not for outstanding citizenship in this world.*

Joe, for example, has a terrible marriage. He and his wife are constantly at loggerheads. They cannot even agree on the proper temperature for tea. Joe contemplates divorce and seeks counsel. His reasons appear irrefutable: Many Christian men have divorced their wives and then lead productive Christian lives. Wouldn't it be better for everyone if he followed their example?

Such an evaluation focuses on what is best for society—that

is, a productive life. For Joe, the command not to divorce his wife is a constant struggle, one that will render him perpetually unproductive—from a human perspective. But from God's perspective, the process of applying the commandment prepares Joe to be a productive member of heaven.

Pete announces that he is changing jobs so that he can be more productive for God, spend more time with his family, and become more involved in ministry. He concludes with the statement, "I have prayed about it, and God is leading me into this new job."

Six months into his new job, Pete is experiencing tension, poor relationships, and unrealistic demands on his time. He concludes, "God is leading me out of this job." Pete's problem is that he is evaluating circumstances on the basis of what he perceives to be productive. He has lost sight of the fact that God is bringing him through the process of preparing him for heaven.

Jesus spent the three years of His public ministry training twelve men to take the good news of His death, burial, and resurrection to the world. Before His death Jesus declared, "I have brought you glory on earth by completing the work you gave me to do" (John 17:4). The finished work to which Jesus referred was the preparation of His disciples; this was the subject of His prayer. He declared to the Father that these men were ready to carry God's truth to a broken humanity.

Clearly, Jesus was talking about a *process*, not a *product*. Just before Jesus' prayer, the mother of James and John came to Him to request that her sons sit on His right and left hands in the kingdom. The response of the other ten was predictable: "They were indignant with the two brothers" (Matthew 20:24). Jesus, in contrast, spoke of spiritual authority and the importance of servanthood.

The boldness of Jesus' declaration that He had completed His work, then, seems to be predicated on the assumption that the work of God is a process. The process of obedience had begun.

The disciples were headed in the right direction, even though the process would take the rest of their lives. Obedience is the process of applying God's Word.

DISOBEDIENCE

If obedience is the process of applying God's word, disobedience is the temporary suspension of that process. Disobedience occurs when a person, by an act of will, either *omits* what God has commanded or *commits* what God has forbidden. David's adultery with Bathsheba, for example, and the murder of her husband were acts of disobedience.

In the opening verses of 2 Samuel 12, when Nathan the prophet confronts David with his sin, David immediately acknowledges his wrong. There is no indication that David tried to justify himself. On the contrary, he records this attitude: "Wash away all my iniquity and cleanse me from my sin. For I know my transgressions, and my sin is always before me. Against you, you only, have I sinned, and done what is evil in your sight, so that you are proved right when you speak and justified when you judge" (Psalm 51:2–4).

David understood that he had sinned, willfully transgressing the command of God. Furthermore, he understood that the sin was not between himself and Bathsheba or Uriah, but between himself and God. This principle is important. If we lose sight of it, we lose sight of the need for obedience. We often try to justify sin against another person, especially if that person has done us wrong; the treachery of the human mind can easily lead us to excuse our mistreatment of another person. Not so with God; since God is just and fair and never sins against us, we never have any excuse for being disobedient to Him.

David never tried to excuse his sin. He never suggested that the commandment of God was unreasonable. He was never confused about that issue. He knew he was in violation of God's law.

How does God feel about disobedience? He hates it, as He hates all sin, but He is willing to forgive it. Realizing that all men are disobedient, God, in Christ Jesus, paid the penalty for that sin by dying on the cross. Paul succinctly states in 2 Corinthians 5:21: "God made him who had no sin to be sin for us, so that in him we might become the righteousness of God."

Disobedience suspends the true application of the Word of God. It is a response contrary to what a person knows to be God's will. Can a person disobey in ignorance? Probably, but that question leads us into an unnecessary theological debate. Application is acting on what we know; we will define disobedience in terms of what a person knows rather than what he or she does not know.

Jeff came to Christ several months ago and carried into his Christian life a lot of unchristian habits. When praying, for example, he frequently swears, not in anger but in the intensity of his emotions. Jeff loves the Lord dearly but has not progressed very far in the process of sanctification.

In contrast, Ralph has known Jesus for many years. He has recently lied to a friend, and God's Spirit has convicted him of that fact, telling him to go and make it right. Embarrassed over his sin and not wanting to "lose his testimony," he resists the Holy Spirit's prompting. Again God's Spirit comes in His convicting power, and again Ralph resists with the excuse that if he resists the Holy Spirit often enough while at the same time expressing his contrition to the Lord, the conviction will go away.

Jeff is obeying while giving the appearance of disobeying. Ralph is disobeying while giving the appearance of obeying. The first man is a delight to God's heart; the second has grieved Him.

REBELLION

If disobedience is the temporary suspension of applying God's Word, rebellion is the redefinition of that process. Rebellion is more than disobedience. King Saul is an illustration. The prophet Samuel came to Saul with instructions from God to destroy Israel's enemies, the Amalekites: "This is what the LORD Almighty says, 'I will punish the Amalekites for what they did to Israel when they waylaid them as they came up from Egypt. Now go, attack the Amalekites and totally destroy everything that belongs to them. Do not spare them; put to death men and women, children and infants, cattle and sheep, camels and donkeys' " (1 Samuel 15:2–3).

Saul was obedient—but only to a point. His army marched against the Amalekites and destroyed them all with the exception of their king, Agag, and the best of their sheep, oxen, and fatlings. Saul intended to take them home and offer them as a sacrifice.

On the return to Israel, Samuel met Saul. Saul's response to the prophet was: "The LORD bless you! I have carried out the LORD's instructions" (1 Samuel 15:13). Amazingly, Saul actually felt he had fulfilled God's commandment. We can only conclude that Saul had so redefined the law that he did not even realize that he had disobeyed it. David was aware that he had sinned; for Saul, that awareness seems to be absent.

Samuel accused Saul of disobedience, and Saul immediately began to blame others for his transgression: "The soldiers brought them from the Amalekites; they spared the best of the sheep and cattle to sacrifice to the LORD your God; but we totally destroyed the rest. . . . I did obey the LORD, . . . I went on the mission the LORD assigned me. I completely destroyed the Amalekites and brought Agag their king. The soldiers took sheep and cattle from the plunder, the best of what was devoted to God, in order to sacrifice them to the LORD your God at Gilgal" (1 Samuel 15:15, 20–21).

Saul did not believe that he had disobeyed God's Word. If Samuel wanted to accuse him of disobedience, Saul was willing to acknowledge a breakdown in communication, as long as the people took the blame. But Samuel was adamant; Saul did wrong. Saul responded: "I have sinned. I violated the LORD's command and your instructions. I was afraid of the people and so I gave in to them. Now I beg you, forgive my sin, and come back with me, so that I may worship the LORD" (1 Samuel 15:24-25).

Saul was cornered into admitting that he did wrong. If Samuel was insistent, Saul was willing to back down. His preoccupation however, was not with his sin, but with his reputation in the eyes of the leaders and people of Israel. "Saul replied, 'I have sinned. But please honor me before the elders of my people and before Israel; come back with me, so that I may worship the LORD your God' " (1 Samuel 15:30).

In verse 24 Saul indicates that he transgressed Samuel's word as well as God's. In verse 25, Samuel is the one who needs to forgive Saul. Saul does not see it as a sin between himself and God. God may be involved, but verse 30 implies that the God of Samuel is angry, not the God of Saul.

Saul's repentance was not motivated by grief over his disobedience toward God, but rather by a sense of personal loss. Both Saul and David did wrong, and both suffered the consequences—David lost the son born to him by Bathsheba (2 Samuel 12:14). But David grieved because he had disobeyed God. Saul grieved because of his own personal loss. Saul was preoccupied with Saul; David was preoccupied with God.

Saul is a perfect example of rebellion. The main aspects of his rebellious life are: (1) a redefinition of the command so that there is no realization of sin; (2) placing the blame on others when there is confrontation; (3) feeling that the breakdown in communication is between himself and another, not sin between himself and God; and (4) being grieved over personal loss rather than over disobedience to God. Samuel understood what was happening and called it rebellion: "Rebellion is like the sin of divination, and arrogance like the evil of idolatry. Because you have rejected the word of the LORD, he has rejected you as king" (1 Samuel 15:23).

Saul's rebellion was overt, but rebellion may be an attitude as well. Passive rebellion is as real as active rebellion, as in the anecdote of the rebellious little boy. When asked by his parents to sit down, he resisted. When commanded to sit, he obeyed. As he sat there with his teeth clenched and a look of defiance on his face, he muttered, "I may be sitting on the outside, but I'm standing on the inside!"

The commandments of God are boundaries around our lives. On occasion, all of us break those boundaries in acts of sin. Disobedience takes place when a person breaks that fence. Rebellion occurs when we begin to challenge the legitimacy or validity of the fence. We come to the fence and ask God if it is wrong to lean on it. If there is nothing wrong with leaning on it, how about putting one arm over it—what about an arm and a leg? Is it permissible to pick up the fence and move it to another location? I may stay on my side of the fence, but I resent it! This is the attitude of rebellion.

People frequently demonstrate this attitude in applying civil law. I may drive on a street at 3 P.M., and the speed limit is 30 miles per hour. The street is congested—school is getting out, and I elect to drive 25 m.p.h. But at 3 A.M., when the same street is vacant, I am tired and eager to get home; then I may drive at 50 m.p.h. even though the speed limit is still 30.

What I have done is to consider the law as something negotiable—not as an absolute, but as something that is relative. I understood the law, took it under advisement, and responded in accordance with what I felt was right. When we do so with God's law, He calls it rebellion. The pattern of rebellion may vary from person to person, but whenever we argue with God over the legitimacy of His commands, we are in rebellion.

Rebellion is taking issue with God regarding his commands, suggesting that they are unreasonable and therefore not legitimate, assuming that the commandments of God are negotiable and redefinable. Rebellion is not only the suspension of the application process, it is the redefinition of that process.

LEGALISM

Obedience has been defined as the process of applying the Word of God. God is interested in the process, even though people are more often interested in the product. Evaluating the product requires measurement and control, and we are never less secure than when we cannot control. Yet the walk of faith requires that we not try to measure and control. There can be no standardization of the *product,* because it is the *process* that is important to God. Legalism, which is the act of defining the process as a product, is an endeavor to walk by sight rather than by faith.

Samuel looked at the outward product rather than the inward process when he went to the sons of Jesse to pick Saul's successor as king of Israel. David's brothers were outwardly attractive, yet God reminded Samuel, "Man looks at the outward appearance, but the LORD looks at the heart" (1 Samuel 16:7). The outward appearance is measurable; the heart is not.

First when we measure, we define the finished product and short-circuit the process. People may be able to live up to certain standards of performance, but this can lull them into believing that they have "arrived" with God. Nothing could be further from the truth.

Second, measurement causes us to compare ourselves with one another. Note the apostle Paul's caution in this regard: "We do not dare to classify or compare ourselves with some who commend themselves. When they measure themselves by themselves and compare themselves with themselves, they are not wise" (2 Corinthians 10:12).

Looking at the body of Christ, we can see people who have embraced an "easy believism." For them, commitment to Christ is a fire-insurance policy rather than a serious commitment to the claims of Christ on their life. They seem to have accepted Jesus as Savior while rejecting Him as Lord.

As desperately as we would like to cull these people from the body of Christ and warn them that they may not be genuine believers, we must resist the temptation. It may be disconcerting that sanctification is a process, but we must remember that when we seek to measure the process or judge a person at any stage in the process, we are tending toward legalism.

Legalism not only seeks to express God's standards solely in terms of measurable attributes, it also tends to set up extrabiblical requirements. Many feel that such activities as dancing and the use of alcoholic beverages are wrong, but these are standards established by man, not by God. God is concerned with our thought life and our purity. Many Christians consider dancing a more serious offense than a biblical prohibition such as engaging a fellow Christian in litigation (1 Corinthians 6).

Unfortunately, many Christians shy away from application out of a fear of legalism. If we look at obedience as the process of applying God's Word, such fears are unfounded. God is not concerned with where we are in the sanctification process compared with other people. He is very interested in what we are doing with what we know. King Josiah stands out as a beautiful illustration of what application is all about. When he heard God's Word, he sought diligently to come to grips with it and apply it in his life.

Nowhere in Scripture does God take a person to task for what he does not know. His short patience is always expressed toward those who know but do not apply.

Simply, obedience is doing what God says. Disobedience is not doing what God says. Rebellion is changing what God says, and legalism is adding to what God says. Obedience is what God desires. Disobedience is a problem of *weakness*, while rebellion and legalism are problems of *willfulness*. In a moment of passion or anger I may be disobedient, but there is no excuse for being willfully rebellious or legalistic.

PRINCIPLES FOR MEDITATION

3. Attitude is as important as action in obeying God's commands.
12. Knowledge carries with it both privilege and responsibility.
13. There is no such thing as a nonessential command.
16. God's permissive will is entered only through a failure to apply the Scriptures.
23. The path to intellectual excellence is curiosity, investigation, and experimentation; but the path to moral excellence is obedience.

QUESTIONS FOR DISCUSSION

1. What are the differences between *disobedience* and *rebellion?* Give at least one illustration for each.
2. What is the difference between *rebellion* and *legalism* ? In which of these two areas do you have the greatest problem?
3. Give an area from your own life where you struggle with each of the three problems: disobedience, rebellion, and legalism.

3 The Process Of Application

God reveals truth to help us become holy saints, not smarter sinners. The command to obey God's Word is based on the premise that revelation requires a response. The Great Commission commands that we teach "all nations to obey" (Matthew 28:20). The heart of a person's relationship with God consists of responding to what the Holy Spirit says. That response is biblical application.

We may be tempted to define the application of God's Word as a "do list." This list may be helpful at times, but we must not lose sight of the objective of application: "Do not conform any longer to the pattern of this world, but be transformed by the renewing of your mind. Then you will be able to test and approve what God's will is—his good, pleasing and perfect will" (Romans 12:2).

Paul states that the focus of application is changing behavior through the renewal of the mind. We will not, therefore, attempt to give a recipe for application or a check list of things to do; rather, we will investigate God's strategy for influencing, remolding, and renewing the mind by exposure to His Word. The "do list" is helpful in the application process but is legitimate only as long as it supports the primary focus of God's strategy— "the renewing of your mind."

RESPONDING TO THE PROCESS

A failure to understand that application is a process can lead to serious error. The great men of God recognized that applying God's Word to their lives was a process, and they worked to stay in that process. They struggled against patterns of behavior and thinking that would take them out of the process. In the Scriptures we find illustrations of both those who stayed in the process and those who dropped out by *manipulating it, presuming on it, and rebelling against it.*

Daniel was a man who understood that he was in the lifelong process of applying God's word. The prophecy of Daniel begins: "In the third year of the reign of Jehoiakim king of Judah, Nebuchadnezzar king of Babylon came to Jerusalem and besieged it. And the Lord delivered Jehoiakim king of Judah into his hand, along with some of the articles from the temple of God. These he carried off to the temple of his god in Babylonia, and put in the treasure house of his god.

"Then the king ordered Ashpenaz, chief of his court officials, to bring in some of the Israelites from the royal family and the nobility" (Daniel 1:1–3).

Daniel was one of the children of Israel taken into captivity at this time. He was removed from his family, his country, his language, and the worship of his God. In Babylon, he was forced to serve the king who was responsible for the captivity of his people, the destruction of his temple, and the annihilation of his beloved city, Jerusalem.

Later, because of his pride, King Nebuchadnezzar was forced to live like an animal for seven years: "Immediately what had been said about Nebuchadnezzar was fulfilled. He was driven away from people and ate grass like cattle. His body was drenched with the dew of heaven until his hair grew like the feathers of an eagle and his nails like the claws of a bird" (Daniel 4:33).

At this time Daniel was prime minister. Certainly he was tempted to do away with this king who was hated by the Jews. With a little imagination one can envision the Jewish leadership urging Daniel to kill the king and take over Babylon. The time was right, and it was obvious that God had placed Nebuchadnezzar in their hands.

But Daniel resisted because he understood that he was involved in a process that belonged to God. He neither rebelled by leaving his post nor manipulated by taking over nor presumed by trying to shorten Nebuchadnezzar's time in the grass. God brought the children of Israel into captivity for their sins; God told the prophet Jeremiah that the captivity would be for seventy years; God put Daniel in a place of significant influence during this seven-year period when Nebuchadnezzar was living like a wild beast. Daniel understood this. It was not his responsibility to take matters into his own hands. He was an obedient participant in the program of God. Consequently, three times God calls him "highly esteemed" (Daniel 9:23; 10:11, 19).

David is a second illustration of a man who understood that applying God's Word is a lifelong process. After the sin of King Saul, Samuel was sent by God to anoint one of the sons of Jesse: "So he sent and had him brought in. He was ruddy, with a fine appearance and handsome features.

"Then the LORD said, 'Rise and anoint him; he is the one.'

"So Samuel took the horn of oil and anointed him in the presence of his brothers, and from that day on the Spirit of the LORD came upon David in power. Samuel then went to Ramah" (1 Samuel 16:12–13).

David knew that he had become the Lord's anointed. Not only did David know, but Saul began to understand it as well. Consequently, Saul sought to kill David, and David fled for his life with Saul in pursuit: "He came to the sheep pens along the way; a cave was there, and Saul went in to relieve himself. David and his men were far back in the cave. The men said, 'This is the very day the LORD spoke of when he said to you, "I will give your enemy into your hands for you to deal with as you wish." ' Then David crept up unnoticed and cut off the corner of Saul's robe.

"Afterward, David was conscience-stricken for having cut off a corner of his robe. He said to his men, 'The LORD forbid that I should do such a thing to my master, the LORD's anointed, or lift my hand against him; for he is the anointed of the LORD' " (1 Samuel 24:3–6).

God had anointed Saul king over Israel. Saul was on the throne. If God wanted Saul off the throne, David knew that God would remove him. It was not David's role to precipitate the action but merely to wait on God's timing. A second time David spared Saul in the Wilderness of Ziph: "So David and Abishai went to the army by night, and there was Saul, lying asleep inside the camp with his spear stuck in the ground near his head. Abner and the soldiers were lying around him.

"Abishai said to David, 'Today God has delivered your enemy into your hands. Now let me pin him to the ground with one thrust of my spear; I won't strike him twice.'

"But David said to Abishai, 'Don't destroy him! Who can lay a hand on the LORD's anointed and be guiltless?' " (1 Samuel 26:7–9).

God anointed Saul; God had to remove Saul. Later, when Saul

THE PROCESS OF APPLICATION

was killed in battle, a man came to David and claimed
responsibility in hope of a reward. Since we know how David felt
about Saul, the response was predictable: "David asked him,
'Why were you not afraid to lift your hand to destroy the LORD's
anointed?'

"Then David called one of his men and said, 'Go, strike him
down!' So he struck him down, and he died. For David had said
to him, 'Your blood be on your own head. Your own mouth
testified against you when you said, 'I killed the LORD's
anointed' " (2 Samuel 1:14–16).

David understood that he was God's servant. God was in
control of David's life, not David. He understood that his
responsibility was to cooperate with God in that process. He was
not to rebel against it, nor was he to try to take matters into his
own hands. David understood that he was in a process.

Rebekah illustrates a person who challenged God's processes
and manipulated events. She was the wife of Isaac and the
mother of twin boys, Jacob and Esau. Before the boys' birth, she
had an encounter with the Lord: "The babies jostled each other
within her, and she said, 'Why is this happening to me?' So she
went to inquire of the LORD.

"The LORD said to her, 'Two nations are in your womb, and
two peoples from within you will be separated; one people will
be stronger than the other, and the older will serve the younger' "
(Genesis 25:22, 23).

Years later, Isaac blesses his two sons (Genesis 27). Rebekah,
fearful that the blessing of the firstborn would go to Esau rather
than Jacob, takes things into her own hands. Because Isaac is old
and almost blind, she is able to deceive him into believing that
Jacob is Esau, so that Jacob steals the blessing that Isaac has
planned for Esau.

God had earlier promised Rebekah that Jacob would receive
the rights of the firstborn, but she felt she needed to manipulate
the process to insure the product. In short, she felt that if God's
promises were true, she had to take things into her own hands.

The results were devastating. Animosity developed between
the brothers; Jacob had to flee for his life and spend the next
twenty years living in a foreign country (Genesis 31:38).
Although the passage does not relate what happened between
Isaac and Rebekah, it probably produced distrust in the marriage. Finally, Rebekah never again saw her favorite son, Jacob.
She died while he was in exile. God finally gave Jacob the
covenant twenty years later at Bethel—as promised.

Joshua is an illustration of a biblical character who was
presumptuous with God. When Joshua became Israel's leader
after Moses' death, God had to encourage him. Joshua undoubt-
edly felt helpless and inadequate to fill the shoes of Moses.

When it was time for Joshua to take the first of the cities,
Jericho, God told him exactly what to do: "See, I have delivered
Jericho into your hands, along with its king and its fighting men.
March around the city once with all the armed men. Do this for
six days. Have seven priests carry trumpets of rams' horns in
front of the ark. On the seventh day, march around the city
seven times, with the priests blowing the trumpets. When you
hear them sound a long blast on the trumpets, have all the people
give a loud shout; then the wall of the city will collapse and the
people will go up, every man straight in" (Joshua 6:2–5).

This conquest was so easy that Joshua felt no need to inquire
of the Lord how to take the next city, Ai: "Now Joshua sent men
from Jericho to Ai, which is near Beth Aven to the east of
Bethel, and told them, 'Go up and spy out the region.' So the
men went up and spied out Ai.

"When they returned to Joshua, they said, 'Not all the people
will have to go up against Ai. Send two or three thousand men to
take it and do not weary all the people, for only a few men are
there.' So about three thousand men went up; but they were
routed by the men of Ai" (Joshua 7:2–4).

Joshua failed to ask the Lord's counsel. If he had, he would
have found out that Achan, one of the children of Israel, had

sinned by taking forbidden booty from Jericho. The Lord's displeasure was expressed in Israel's defeat at Ai.

Chagrined by the setback, Joshua brought the problem of Ai to the Lord. Soon, Ai was taken, and the inhabitants of Gibeon came to Joshua, pretending to be from a far country: "The men of Israel sampled their provisions *but did not inquire of the LORD*. Then Joshua made a treaty of peace with them to let them live, and the leaders of the assembly ratified it by oath" (Joshua 9:14–15, emphasis ours).

This passage illustrates presumption. Joshua presumed on the promise that they would conquer the land, and he did not bring the critical issue of Gibeon before God. Similarly, we presume on God when we decide on a course of action without first going to God in prayer and to the Word.

Jonah rebelled against the process. The Book of Jonah begins with these words: "The word of the LORD came to Jonah son of Amittai: 'Go to the great city of Nineveh and preach against it, because its wickedness has come up before me' " (Jonah 1:1–2).

Jonah understood that God was gracious, but he was displeased with God's application of His grace. Nineveh was the capital of Assyria, one of Israel's worst enemies. The idea that the grace of God would be lavished on Israel's enemy was more than Jonah could handle.

Jonah's rebellion took him out to sea in the opposite direction of Nineveh, where he faced a storm, was thrown overboard, was swallowed by a great fish, and eventually was spit out upon the land. Finally convinced that he could not ignore the will of God, he preached repentance to the city of Nineveh. Then Jonah's worst apprehensions were fulfilled; Nineveh repented, and God forgave them. But "Jonah was greatly displeased and became angry. He prayed to the LORD, 'O LORD, is this not what I said when I was still at home? That is why I was so quick to flee to Tarshish. I knew that you are a gracious and compassionate God, slow to anger and abounding in love, a God who relents from sending calamity" (Jonah 4:1–2).

Jonah loved God's grace but rebelled over His dispersal of it. These are the various ways we can respond to the application process. We can be willing participants; or we can manipulate, presume, or rebel.

THE FOUR PHASES OF PROCESS

Scripture indicates four distinct phases in applying God's Word: recognition, response, results, and reward.

Recognition: Before the process of applying the Word can begin, we must recognize who we are in God's eyes. Obedience is essential in a person's relationship with God. The impact of this truth, however, is related to our understanding of *who we are* and *how we fit into God's program.* To put it another way, our recognition of our need to apply God's Word is an outgrowth of our understanding of our purpose for being here on earth.

Our city has an annual 10,000-meter race. It has become a popular event with more than 25,000 participants each year. Last July was unusually hot, and many runners became ill and dropped out before completing the race. A friend of ours, one of the dropouts, confessed to two problems: first, he did not have the right attitude in preparation, and second, he trained with the wrong people. His buddies were not training to be finishers. Consequently, although he compared favorably with them, he was inadequately prepared for the meet.

The same principle applies in preparing for the application process. If we do not recognize who we are, we will compare ourselves with others, be ill prepared for life's race, and miss our goal of godliness.

Thinking people wrestle with the question "Who am I?" From a biblical perspective, however, the more pressing question is, "*Whose* am I?" Who I am is directly related to "to whom do I belong?" In the Scriptures, our need for application is tied to our belonging to God.

The Sermon on the Mount reflects the application process.

The first three Beatitudes demonstrate "recognition": "Blessed are the poor in spirit, for theirs is the kingdom of heaven. Blessed are those who mourn, for they will be comforted. Blessed are the meek, for they will inherit the earth" (Matthew 5:3–5).

The "poor in spirit" understand who they are in God's sight. They are "beggarly in spirit," an attitude that grows out of realizing their utter helplessness. We come to God with nothing but complete emptiness.

The "mourning" of verse 4 is sorrow for sin—true contrition, mourning for both self and others. Such mourning for others is not pity, which is feeling sorry for others because they do not have what we have. Because we see ourselves as God sees us, we are "beggarly of spirit" and "mourn" for our own helpless condition and hence the condition of others.

These two Beatitudes lead to the third—"meekness." This *controlled strength* is a kind of humility that leads to gentleness, patience, teachability: dependence on God for our self-worth.

These three qualities—poverty of spirit, mourning, meekness—prepare a person for a life of application. Apart from this, a person will pursue self-serving interests because he or she depends on others for self-worth. God wants us to look to Him rather than to others. If we do not see ourselves from God's perspective, we will respond to people's expectations rather than to God's Word, and thereby distort the application process.

Not only do we need to know who (and whose) we are, we also need to know how we fit into God's program. Understanding our purpose for existence is important in "recognition." Knowledge of purpose gives life meaning, value, and fulfillment. God does not hide our purpose from us. As the Westminster Catechism says: "The chief end of man is to glorify God and enjoy Him forever." If we understand that, then the need for application will be clear.

Terry, an upright successful businessman, has come to peace

with the question "who am I?" by defining his existence in terms of the world. Because he does not know God and admits no need of Him, he does not participate in the process of biblical application. If change takes place in Terry's life, it comes in response to people's expectations rather than God's.

The beginning of the application process is the recognition of who we are and what our purpose is.

Response: When my son was learning to drive, we took a trip into the country. The road was familiar to me; I had negotiated it on numerous occasions. Among the curves, one was especially bad; hidden from sight at the top of a knoll, the unbanked curve was difficult to handle. My son and I had rehearsed the perils of this curve, and as we made our way down the road, various road signs supported my caution. But the approach seemed deceptively harmless, and he chose to follow his instincts rather than his dad's admonition and the signs' warning. The result was an afternoon spent in the ditch.

Many people respond to the Scriptures that way. Ignoring fellow Christians' counsel and the road signs in the Bible, they follow their own instincts.

In our saner moments we know that we need to respond in obedience to the Scriptures. Unfortunately, our thinking has been shaped by our culture rather than by the Bible; Paul warns, "Do not conform any longer to the pattern of this world, but be transformed by the renewing of your mind" (Romans 12:2). As we filter our culture through the Bible rather than the Bible through our culture, we begin to think God's thoughts and, consequently, begin to live a godly life.

In the Sermon on the Mount, Beatitudes 4–7 deal with "response": "Blessed are those who hunger and thirst for righteousness, for they will be filled. Blessed are the merciful, for they will be shown mercy. Blessed are the pure in heart, for they will see God. Blessed are the peacemakers, for they will be called sons of God" (Matthew 5:6–9).

Without responding to God's truth the heart becomes dull and hardened, and the application process ends. James notes in his epistle: "Any one who listens to the word but does not do what it says is like a man who looks at his face in a mirror and, after looking at himself, goes away and immediately forgets what he looks like" (James 1:23–24). As James points out, non-response produces non-growth, and for this reason many Christians remain spiritually immature all their lives.

The process of growth would be streamlined, of course, if we could find a simple technique for responding properly to God's Word. But obedience is acting on what the Holy Spirit says, and the direction of such action is often varied. *How* one responds cannot be codified. The response itself is an act of faith.

The Bible teaches that the Holy Spirit reveals truth so there will be application (Matthew 13:11–17). As the believer applies the truth of God's Word, His Spirit reveals more. We may know only a little, but we are expected to act upon what we know. Refusal to act ends the process; God's Spirit hides further truth from the person who resists obedience. The mind's renewal is essential for application, and the Holy Spirit will not assist in the renewal process unless the heart is committed to application. In short, the Holy Spirit will not convict our hearts with new truths merely to increase knowledge. He expects us to act on it.

Results: In chemistry, a number of signs can indicate that a reaction is in process. When iron and sulfuric acid are mixed, the odor of rotten eggs is not the final product, nor does it indicate how close the process is to completion; but it does show that something is happening. Similarly, in the application process, as we *respond*, we can expect "the fragrance of Christ"—not as the *reward* of application, but as the *feedback* of the process of becoming Christlike.

This third phase in applying God's Word (after recognition and response) is seeing the results. God in His infinite grace has allowed us *feedback* as we endeavor to respond properly to

Scripture's teachings: "Do not conform any longer to the pattern of this world, but be transformed by the renewing of your mind. Then you will be able to test and approve what God's will is— his good, pleasing and perfect will" (Romans 12:2).

By being transformed rather than conformed, we demonstrate "that the plan of God for you is good, meets all his demands and moves toward the goal of true maturity" (Romans 12:2 PHILLIPS). Second Peter 1:8 reminds us that if the characteristics mentioned in the preceding verses are set into motion in life, "they will keep you from being ineffective and unproductive." Such results indicate that we are progressing.

John 2:22 illustrates God's use of feedback in helping His disciples: "After he was raised from the dead, his disciples recalled what he had said. Then they believed the Scripture and the words that Jesus had spoken." Raising Jesus from the dead was the feedback that God's Spirit gave the disciples, causing them to believe both the Scriptures and the Lord's words. This was not intended to make them think they were mature or finished, but rather to enhance their involvement in the process of maturity with a deeper commitment to the authority of the Word.

In the Sermon on the Mount, Jesus says that our feedback will come from two directions. First, we will experience persecution and rejection: "Blessed are those who are persecuted because of righteousness, for theirs is the kingdom of heaven. Blessed are you when people insult you, persecute you and falsely say all kinds of evil against you because of me" (Matthew 5:10–11).

Second, we will be salt and light: "You are the salt of the earth. But if the salt loses its saltiness, how can it be made salty again? It is no longer good for anything, except to be thrown out and trampled by men.

"You are the light of the world. A city on a hill cannot be hidden. Neither do people light a lamp and put it under a bowl. Instead they put it on its stand, and it gives light to everyone in the house. In the same way let your light shine before men, that they may see your good deeds and praise your Father in heaven" (Matthew 5:13–16). The feedback in verse 16 is the response to God. People see our "good works," but the glory does not go to us, but to our "Father in heaven."

The results, or feedback, will always be in accordance with the Scriptures' promises and will always result in God's glory. We can never *measure* our achievement with God with the feedback; God's promises will be mostly qualitative, manifesting themselves in such results as the "fruit of the Spirit" (Galatians 5:22–23).

Failure to view properly the results of application will distort the process and lead a person into manipulation or presumption. Feedback should always drive us to a closer relationship with God, make us more committed to the Word, and cause us to glorify Him.

Mrs. Vander Grump is a faithful member and worker in the Reformed Dispensational Baptist Church. She teaches Sunday school, does special projects in the church office, and drives the handicapped to and from church. If you ask her, she will tell you that she is doing these things for the cause of Christ, and in fact, she may tell you even if you do not ask. Her feelings are hurt if the pastor does not periodically sing her praises from the pulpit. She seeks feedback from people rather than God, for the glory of Mrs. Vander Grump.

The biblical promise of results or feedback seems to conflict with the need to walk by faith. Many of the rewards of obedience accrue in eternity rather than on earth. Because the Lord knows our frailty and understands our need for encouragement, He periodically reveals the fruit of our labor to assure us that we are moving in the right direction.

Reward: The fourth and final phase in the application process is reward, a promised reward that is eternal. Even when there are immediate results in applying the Scriptures, these should not detract from our focus on the eternal results. Jesus called attention to this: "Do not store up for yourselves treasures on earth, where moth and rust destroy, and where thieves break in and steal. But store up for yourselves treasures in heaven, where moth and rust do not destroy, and where thieves do not break in and steal. For where your treasure is, there your heart will be also" (Matthew 6:19–21).

In John, the Lord reiterates: "Do not let your hearts be troubled. Trust in God; trust also in me. In my Father's house are many rooms; if it were not so, I would have told you. I am going there to prepare a place for you. And if I go and prepare a place for you, I will come back and take you to be with me that you also may be where I am" (John 14:1–3). The same emphasis is seen in the Sermon on the Mount: "Rejoice and be glad, because great is your reward in heaven" (Matthew 5:12).

Jesus said that our reward will be found not here but in heaven. If those rewards are not properly understood, we, like Mrs. Vander Grump, will begin to manipulate circumstances, to look to people's recognition rather than to God's promises for our encouragement. The process will then be distorted and unfulfilling.

Implications: The rest of the Sermon on the Mount deals with the implications of these four phases in the application process—*recognition, response, results,* and *reward.* In Matthew 5:17–48, Jesus evaluates the results of being product-oriented rather than process-oriented. The Pharisees' handling of the law affords an illustration. Because they were product-oriented, they viewed themselves as righteous, as *the* standard. In Matthew 5:48 Jesus reminds us that if we want to look for a standard of righteousness, then we must at least pick the right one—"Be perfect, therefore, as your heavenly Father is perfect." The wrong standard will lead us to breach the process by rebellion. Acceptance of the right standard is the first step in the recognition phase.

Next, in Matthew 6:1–18, Jesus reviews ceremony and worship. He deals with people who have the wrong motive or look to others for recognition and reward rather than to heaven, those who make feedback the reward. In so doing, we breach the process by presumption.

Finally, in Matthew 6:19–34, Jesus discusses the need to look to God rather than to people to meet our needs. To violate this will lead us to breach the process by manipulation.

A QUESTION OF PERSPECTIVE

Application is a four-phase process: recognition, response, results, and reward. But application as a process can only be properly understood in contrast to application as a product. Most people are product-oriented and ask, "What are the results?" "What is the bottom line?" "How will this net out?"

Phase three in the application process is "results." God does promise us feedback, and positive feedback results in encouragement. Our tendency, however, is to expect this encouragement at every step, and then to become product-oriented, rather than process-oriented. Instead of walking by faith, we begin to walk by sight.

When a student studies math, for example, he or she works on a difficult problem, then turns to the back of the book for the answer. The answer in the the book is the feedback to let the student know if he or she is doing the problem correctly. Soon, however, the student begins turning to the back of the book first, and forgets that the point of the exercise is to learn rather than to get the correct answer. The grade is no longer an indicator of progress but a key to acceptance and personal worth.

The same is true of our relationship with God. The Lord occasionally gives us results to let us know that we are headed in the right direction. Our culture, however, teaches us that the results are an end in themselves rather than a means to an end. If believers are not careful, they can forget that they are in a process produced by God to prepare them for the time they will give an account for the way they responded to that process.

As soon as we begin to focus on the feedback, we lose sight of what our relationship with God ought to be. We cease to respond to His revelation and begin, rather, to respond to results. Herein lies the breakdown in the application process. God never promised the believer "blessings" as the world evaluates them. Often the believer's lot in life is pain, misunderstanding, rejection, and persecution. The believer's hope is not in this world, but in what God promises in the world to come. The person who succumbs to the temptation to "turn to the back of the book" jeopardizes the entire application process.

PRINCIPLES FOR MEDITATION

5. Application is a process, not a single event.
19. The difference between a trial and a temptation lies in the response.

QUESTIONS FOR DISCUSSION

1. Define or describe the process of application.
2. Assuming that you are not always an eager participant in the application process can you most easily identify with: Rebekah, Jonah, or Joshua? Elaborate.
3. There are four phases in the application process: recognition, response, results, and reward. Define these four phases, pointing out their differences.

II The Process of Application

Note: in this section, we will talk about the various questions that must be addressed if you are going to engage in a lifelong process of applying the Scriptures. These are critical issues that deal with the way you face life. Don't try to read them with the idea of "knowing" what they say or trying to glean from them a mechanical list of how-to's. You will know that you have adequately responded to the content when you have prayerfully assimilated their truths and submitted to them. To the degree that you hve done this, you can be assured that you are a willing participant in the application process through which God is bringing you. Conversely, if there are portions of these chapters that cause you to stumble, somewhere in the application process you will stumble.

The material in this section is not easy to assimilate. You may want to read some portions several times. In delving into it, however, know that you are addressing the six key issues of application.

4 The Filter Is Foundational to Change

A friend and I were visiting a family in the Orient. Before us lay a sumptuous meal carefully prepared by our hostess. At the center of the table was a large fish, the head intact. The eye was looking straight at us, the teeth displaying a fishy grin. As we gathered around the table, the host stood between my friend and me to insure that we were properly cared for.

He reached over and cut off the fish head, placing it before my friend with the words, "We would like you, as our guest of honor, to have the choicest serving." As this scene unfolded, I wondered how he was going to eat it. I broke into a cold sweat at the thought that he might want to share it with me.

My friend stood and walked over to the hostess at the opposite side of the table. He placed the fish head before her and said, "In our country we always serve the hostess the most delicate portion." I marveled at his ability to think quickly and then began to ponder what had transpired. If I had been raised as a child in that family, I would have found my salivary glands secreting instead of my stomach churning. The food was not the point, but rather my perception of what constituted *good* food.

FILTER SYSTEMS

How we have been conditioned to perceive fish heads affects how we view them. When we look at reality—food, nature, people, events, or the truth of the Bible—our ability to see it clearly is affected by the environment in which we have been raised—our filter system. This is made up of circumstances that enter our lives from the moment of birth. Reality is seen through that filter; the filter system affects all our perceptions.

The filter is dynamic, not static. Because new circumstances and experiences are constantly entering our lives, our filter, or grid, is in a perpetual state of change. We do not perceive things today the same way we did ten years ago, nor will we see them ten years from now the way we do today.

This filter system, or world view, is made up of certain assumptions, and is shaped by four major influences in our lives:

Social Structure. The type of family from which a person comes plays a decisive role in the development of his or her world view. A close-knit family, a broken home, the neighborhood, the family's social values, all play a part.

A young girl whose father was an alcoholic, for example, is affected all her life by her experience. Daily he arrived home drunk, beat her mother, and intimidated the children. One day he died. The mother wanted nothing to do with men and communicated her lack of trust to her daughter. We do not need great insight to suspect that when the young girl reaches the age of twenty, her experience will affect her view of men as she contemplates marriage.

Economic Values. A person's background in a free-enterprise society or a socialist system affects that person's filter. Those raised in and committed to a *laissez-faire* view of economics find themselves shocked by the violent reaction of people who have embraced socialism. Not simply one's personal experience causes such views to be polarized, but also the environment in which one is raised—the sense of values instilled from the moment of birth.

A young couple, for example, fell in love and married. He came from a family of entrepreneurs. His father had made and lost three fortunes; "easy come, easy go." She came from a family where the investment of every dollar is a major event. Her family never had much and sought to hold on to what they had. It is not difficult to see that this couple will have to make adjustments in their marriage.

Politics. In Latin America, an intelligent young Christian worker was asked what form of government was ideal from his perspective. His response—a benevolent dictatorship—may come as a shock to those of us who were raised believing in the American Declaration of Independence and the Bill of Rights.

Religion. One's world view is nowhere more clearly seen than in religion. Strong convictions about God and His will have been behind some of the greatest atrocities man has committed. Two people can read the same Bible, pray to the same God, and arrive at entirely different conclusions. This is the stuff of which denominations are made.

The formation of a person's grid, or filter system, could be diagrammed like this:

Applied to lay ministry these three filters will affect our grids in terms of:

1. *What we believe to be possible.* Do we believe it is possible to entrust the ministry to those who have not been theologically trained? Do we believe it is possible for them to minister the sacraments and start churches without chaos resulting?

I	II	III	GRID

P
E   What he   What he
R   believes to   actually   What he
S   be possible   experiences   reflects on
O
N

2. *What we actually experience.* Have we ever actually seen such a ministry? What did it look like? Will our filters allow us to consider it a success?

3. *What we reflect on.* What does the Bible teach regarding a lay ministry? Have we ever taken time to study the subject? Where is God at work, and what does He seem to be blessing?

Our grid is made up of assumptions, most of which have never been proven. We have strong convictions about such subjects as individualism, democracy, justice, labor unions, education, liquor, and patriotism, but we often have never taken time to study, think through, or prove our conclusions. We simply believe what we do about them.

Each person's experience is interpreted by a world view and the assumptions that form it. In our culture, for example, if I have a stomach ache, I go to the doctor. He diagnoses it as a bacterial infection and prescribes an antibiotic. Three days later I feel better and conclude the doctor cured me. Or if I feel worse, I conclude that the doctor had misdiagnosed it. It was probably a virus.

In another culture, with the same stomach ache, I might go to a witch doctor. He diagnoses that I have an evil spirit. Through a ritual he casts out the evil spirit, and three days later I feel well and conclude that the witch doctor did a good job. Or if I feel worse, I conclude that the evil spirit was stronger than the witch doctor suspected.

In still another culture, I am afflicted with the same problem and go to the priest for help. He thinks my soul is sick and offers a sacrifice. Three days later I feel better and conclude that the priest was able to propitiate the gods. Or if I feel worse, I conclude that my soul is sicker than the priest imagined.

In all three instances the experience—whether positive or negative—*confirms* the validity of the world view. One's grid influences the perception and understanding of not only what *is* happening and what *does* happen but also what *can* happen.

FILTER SYSTEMS AND THE BIBLE

John 11 records the raising of Lazarus from the dead. When Jesus asks that the stone covering the grave be removed, Martha remarked, "But, Lord, . . . by this time there is a bad odor, for he has been there four days" (v. 39). With the multitudes watching, Jesus raised the decaying body of Lazarus to life. In response "many of the Jews who had come to visit Mary, and had seen what Jesus did, put their faith in him. But some of them went to the Pharisees and told them what Jesus had done" (John 11:45–46).

It staggers the imagination that some could watch this miracle and respond negatively—until we ponder the powerful influence of the filter system. We can postulate five different assumptions regarding miracles and see where they lead us:

1. *Assumption:* God does not exist. *Conclusion:* Miracles cannot happen.

2. *Assumption:* God exists, but He is distant and unconcerned with the affairs of man. *Conclusion:* Miracles could happen, but they do not.

3. *Assumption:* God exists, but as a philosophical concept that plays a part in those segments of life designated as "religious." *Conclusion:* People once thought that miracles happened, but

now we explain such things scientifically and marvel at how
naïve people could be.

4. *Assumption:* God is very active in human affairs. *Conclusion:* Miracles are continually happening all around us.

5. *Assumption:* The form of God's activity in human affairs
varies from age to age. *Conclusion:* Miracles are seasonal. They
can be seen in the times of Moses, Judges, Elijah and Elisha, the
Lord Jesus, and the early church, but are dormant at other times.
Currently we are in a dormant period.

Most Christians embrace assumption 4 or 5. At precisely this
point the division between charismatic and noncharismatic views
can be seen. One sees God's activity in our lives today—
especially in the distribution of spiritual gifts—differently than
the other. It is a difference of world view.

The difference isn't necessarily one of Scripture's inspiration.
Two people can have the same view on the Bible's inerrancy and
authority, and interpret the Bible in different ways.

Immediately after becoming a believer, I was zealous in my
Christian witness and consequently developed the reputation at
my college of knowing a lot about the Bible. Actually the
opposite was true. I scarcely knew the difference between the
Old and New Testaments. One night four students, thoroughly
inebriated, entered my room to argue religion. One of the four
claimed to be a Christian because he had gone forward in a
meeting and was baptized. His lifestyle was no different from the
other three, and they disputed his claim. I was to be the
arbitrator. So I suggested that if baptism were the key to the
Kingdom of Heaven, I could pull the fire alarm, and we could
throw the students into the swimming pool as they came out of
the building. Then we would evangelize the campus in short
order.

They laughed and staggered out of the room. On reflection, I
concluded that baptism was a hindrance to the Gospel. Later I
read 1 Corinthians 1:14–17: "I am thankful that I did not baptize

any of you except Crispus and Gaius, so no one can say that you were baptized into my name. (Yes, I also baptized the household of Stephanas; beyond that I don't remember if I baptized anyone else.) For Christ did not send me to baptize, but to preach the gospel—not with words of human wisdom, lest the cross of Christ be emptied of its power.''

That sealed it. The Bible taught what I had already suspected. Not only was baptism unnecessary, it was a hindrance. This understanding of baptism was, of course, fallacious. But it wasn't until my world view on the subject changed that I changed.

Not only do people differ on what the Bible says, but they also differ on the relative importance of what the Bible says. One fellowship emphasizes the importance of personal holiness and separation from the world; in another, the accent is on God's sovereignty; in still another the social implications of the Bible are stressed. These differences illustrate the presence of a grid in all of our lives.

An illustration from Jesus' life indicates the presence of a filter system in all of our lives: "On reaching Jerusalem, Jesus entered the temple area and began driving out those who were buying and selling there. He overturned the tables of the moneychangers and the benches of those selling doves, and would not allow anyone to carry merchandise through the temple courts. And as he taught them he said, 'Is it not written: "My house will be called a house of prayer for all nations"? But you have made it a "den of robbers." ''

"The chief priests and the teachers of the law heard this and began looking for a way to kill him, for they feared him, because the whole crowd was amazed at his teaching" (Mark 11:15–18).

In verse 17 Jesus was quoting Isaiah 56:7 to show the Jewish religious leaders how they had misused God's temple. From Jesus' perspective, through His filter system, He saw that the temple was being abused.

The first part of verse 18 gives us the understanding of what transpired through the the religious leaders' grid. They did not feel that they were misusing the temple, concluded that Jesus' teaching was a threat, and sought to eliminate Him.

Finally, at the end of verse 18, we have the third perception of what took place. Like the religious leaders, the people had not realized that they were misusing the temple; they, however, were amazed at Jesus' teaching on the subject and sought to change their filter system. When we hear God's Word, we either react like these religious leaders and reject it for one reason or another, or we react like the people who stand in amazement over what is being said and allow it to alter our own filter system.

FILTER SYSTEMS AND APPLICATION

Most of us tend to think of application as a set of "do lists." As we read God's Word and have our hearts sensitized by the Holy Spirit, we are led to put into practice our Lord's commands and admonitions. Although the "do list" is an integral part of application, it is not the heart of the application process.

The apostle Paul gave a clue concerning the focus of application. In Romans 8:29 he talks about being conformed to the likeness of Christ. He is obviously not talking about physical features but rather about a person's value system: how he or she perceives life—in short, the altering of one's filter system.

All of us act on the basis of what we see, that is, how we perceive things as they filter through our grids. Our filter systems affect perception, and our perception affects application. *Thus all permanent change in a person's life begins with a change in perspective.* To be conformed to the likeness of Christ is to think God's thoughts after him, to see things through His grid.

The Bible talks about "being" and "doing." In Romans 12:2 Paul exhorts, "*Do* not conform any longer to the pattern of this world, but *be* transformed by the renewing of your mind" (emphasis ours). James 1:22 says, "Do not merely listen to the word, . . . *do* what it says" (emphasis ours).

The person who *does* majors on the "do list" in application. Those who concentrate on *being* focus on the filter system. This is not to suggest that the two are mutually exclusive, rather they are mutually inclusive. *Being,* however, comes before *doing.* Doing is the product of being, not vice versa. A person can do the right thing without permanent change taking place in his or her life. Or a person can attend church regularly, do what he or she is told, participate in all the functions of the church, and never see appreciable change taking place in his or her life.

When a person majors on *being,* however, the doing naturally follows. A person cannot be what God wants without doing what God asks; the two are inclusive. The application process centers on what a person is rather than what he or she does.

Because all of us have a world view through which we filter experience, we tend to filter God's word through our cultural grid as well. We then find ourselves confirmed in our own presuppositions rather than being "transformed by the renewing of our minds." Thus the socialist, the capitalist, those who practice apartheid, and the abolitionist all see their position trumpeted in the Scriptures. A person can listen to the preaching of the Word Sunday after Sunday with minimal change taking place in his or her life, simply because that person filters God's Word through a cultural grid. The proclaimed Word simply confirms what was already believed.

How, then, is change to take place? We can facilitate change through a threefold process:

1. *We need to recognize the presence of filter systems in our lives.* All of us have a grid, but not all of us realize it. We must realize that we perceive reality through a grid composed of social structure, economic values, politics, and religion.

2. *We should be suspicious of the validity of our cultural grid.* Certainly, everything our culture teaches us is not wrong, but it is not to be accepted without evaluation. Much of what our culture teaches is good—or at least neutral—but a great deal of

it does not accord with biblical teaching. As we expose ourselves to God's Word, we must recognize that the grid exists. And we must be willing to challenge it.

3. *We must insist that we filter our culture through God's Word rather than filtering God's Word through our cultural grid.* None of us can do this perfectly. It is a lifelong process that produces change and leads toward sanctification. Even though this process is difficult and inadequately executed, it is essential for "being conformed into the image of Christ." Altering the filter system according to God's Word is the process whereby we are "transformed by the renewing of our minds."

PRINCIPLES FOR MEDITATION

12. Knowledge carries with it both privilege and responsibility.
13. There is no such thing as a nonessential command.
14. We must not insist that we will obey only after a seeming contradiction in commandments is resolved.
19. Culture cannot serve as an excuse for not obeying God's commands.

QUESTIONS FOR DISCUSSION

1. Give several illustrations of filters in others' lives.
2. Give one or two illustrations of where the filter is present in your life.
3. Explain in your own words the correlation between the filter system and the *process* of application.

SOURCES

Dr. Charles Kraft. *Anthropology—M630.* Class at Fuller Theological Seminary, School of World Missions.

Neal Postman and Charles Weingartner. *Teaching as a Subversive Activity.* Delta Books.

Louis J. Luzbetak. *The Church and Cultures.* William Carey Library, 1970.

Risk Taking

The heart of the application process is expressed by Paul: "Do not conform any longer to the pattern of this world, but be transformed by the renewing of your minds" (Romans 12:2). This involves the realignment of our cultural grids so that we see things from a biblical perspective.

As simple and obvious as this may seem, it is extremely difficult in practice. Our world view is very dear to us. Any tampering with it causes trauma, as when society calls into question traditional values or standards. When people live in a foreign country they find that the more different the culture, the more difficult the adjustment.

Romans 12:2 is a command requiring an act of the will. The

transformation of the mind does not happen by osmosis; questioning one's cultural grid requires an act of the will simply because it is an uncomfortable process. To align one's life with what the Bible teaches is threatening and, therefore, requires *risk taking*.

BIBLICAL FAITH

Hebrews 11, the great chapter on biblical faith, can be broken into three parts: Explanation of faith (verses 1–3), examples of faith (verses 4–31), exploits of faith (verses 32–40).[1]

The author of Hebrews defines faith as "being sure of what we hope for and certain of what we do not see" (Hebrews 11:1).

Faith can be demonstrated in only two areas—in what we do not see, the invisible; and in what we hope for, the future. Unless something is either invisible or in the future, it cannot require faith. Faith is the guarantee of the future and the proof of the invisible. Commitment comes before knowledge. You cannot know the validity of your commitment until after you have committed yourself, or as Augustine put it: "I believe, therefore I know."

I go to the physician. He diagnoses my illness, scratches a prescription on a piece of paper, and hands it to me. I cannot understand his marks, but I take the prescription to the pharmacist. He looks at it, nods, goes to work, puts some pills in a bottle, hands it to me, and I take them as directed. That is commitment before knowledge.

This kind of faith is synonymous with risk taking. The object of risk taking determines what we call it. If, for example, the object of our risk taking is dice, we call it gambling. If the object of our risk taking is the stock market, we call it business. If the object of our risk taking is God, we call it biblical faith. All of these demand commitment before knowledge. All of them demand risk taking.

---

[1] For a more thorough look at Hebrews 11, see *After the Sacrifice* by Walter A. Henrichsen, Zondervan Publishing.

THE PURPOSE OF FAITH

It is impossible to live without risk; God has woven the need to walk by faith into the very fabric of existence. Every time we cross the street, drive an automobile, fly in an airplane, eat food, we are committing ourselves before knowing. Faith is not unique to Christianity, it is part of living—something that all people, Christian and non-Christian alike, must do.

The root of sin is man's declaration of independence. When Adam and Eve ate the forbidden fruit in the Garden of Eden, they declared their independence from God. Any reconciliation with God, therefore, begins with renunciation of that independence—in short, it begins with living life dependent upon God.

To teach humans their need for dependence on God, He made faith, or risk taking, an integral part of existence; it is a question of what or who we are going to trust. Trusting God is important because it acknowledges our dependence on Him. He has asked us to take risks. Every time we have to commit ourselves before knowing, we are registering our dependence on Him.

WALKING BY FAITH IS UNCOMFORTABLE

Because walking by faith is commitment before knowledge, none of us likes to do it. Some people see themselves as risk takers and seem to enjoy the adventure and excitement. But even for such people, the willingness to commit before knowing occurs outside the limits of their comfort zone. For every person, there are areas of life that constitute "unacceptable" risks.

Scientifically, knowing God's will is impossible, just as it is impossible to know that the Bible is God's Word, that heaven and hell exist, and that Jesus is the Son of God. We "know" these things only in the sense that, by faith, we have committed ourselves to their truth. From the scientific perspective we don't know them; we simply believe them. If we were able to know them, we would not need faith. But God says that without faith it is impossible to please Him (Hebrews 11:6).

Because walking by faith is so uncomfortable, all of us seek to minimize our risks: the businessman investing his money; a mother taking care before giving birth to a child; the Christian seeking to walk in God's will. God encourages us to minimize our risks through what can be called "subjective indicators" and "objective indicators."

1. *Subjective Indicators*. When two people get married, how do they know they have chosen the right spouse? Nowhere does the Bible say, "Thou shalt marry Jane," or "Thou shalt marry Bill." Assuming they want to marry the right person, that is, the person of God's choice, how do they minimize their risks? They can seek counsel from godly people; they can commit the decision to prayer; and they can follow the Holy Spirit's lead as He either gives them peace or the lack of it in their courtship.[2]

These are all *subjective* indicators of what they should do. None of these, however, eliminate risk. When people go for counsel, they often want somebody else to make their decisions for them. They would like to shift the risk from themselves to someone else. Then, if the situation doesn't work out, it is the fault of the person who gave the counsel.

2. *Objective Indicators*. The objective indicators are the commands and promises found in God's word. Because we believe the Bible to be God's Word, we accept its statements as true. In salvation, for example, I do not consider myself a Christian because of my feelings. If I did, I would be open to vacillation and despair, for my feelings vary from moment to moment and from day to day. I do not consider myself a Christian because other people say I am. They may be wrong. No, I consider myself a Christian because the Bible says, "Everyone who calls on the name of the Lord will be saved"

---

[2]Subjective and objective indicators will be discussed more thoroughly in Chapter 8, "The Source of Application."

(Romans 10:13); and "If you confess with your mouth, 'Jesus is Lord' and believe in your heart that God raised him from the dead, you will be saved" (Romans 10:9). I base my salvation on God's Word. Although I do not know (in a scientific sense) that when I die I am going to heaven, my commitment and trust is that these words are true, and my actions correspond to that commitment.

In both the subjective and objective indicators, the need to walk by faith is not eliminated. In both, commitment before knowledge is necessary.

A person's willingness to take risks is dependent on how badly he or she wants to know. For example, I am willing to take the medicine the doctor prescribes because I feel so bad that I would rather take the risk of swallowing the wrong pill than to continue in my misery. Christianity is a religion of rescue, designed for the desperate. The willingness to commit to Christ is predicated on the need for what God has promised, or as Jesus said, "It is not the healthy who need a doctor, but the sick. I have not come to call the righteous, but sinners to repentance" (Luke 5:31).

APPLICATION

Application implies the transformation of one's filter system. Because we cannot know God's will in a scientific sense, and because commitment comes before knowledge, commitment to obeying the Scriptures appears to be a tremendous risk. Application is risk taking.

One of the most dynamic aspects of faith is application. To allow the Scriptures to alter our cultural filter system is very threatening because the change that the Scripture requires is a radical demand that often appears illogical, inconsistent, and ill-defined.

1. *Illogical.* Christ's claims are reasonable but not logical. He tells those who follow Him that the secret of living is dying. If we want to save our lives, we must lose them. The path to being first

is being last. Those who want to be leaders must accomplish their goal by being servants. Giving is the secret to getting; we should invest in the unseen rather than the seen. These commands are the antithesis of the world's value system; from a worldly perspective, a person would be foolish to commit to them.

Worldly logic has a tremendous influence on us and, if we are not careful, will cause us to be selective in applying God's Word. God warns: "My thoughts are not your thoughts, neither are your ways my ways" (Isaiah 55:8). Jesus said, "You are the ones who justify yourselves in the eyes of men, but God knows your hearts. What is highly valued among men is detestable in God's sight" (Luke 16:15).

2. *Inconsistent.* The Scriptures sometimes appear to be inconsistent, as in the case of the "seeming paradoxes" of Christ's deity and His humanity, or God's sovereignty and man's responsibility. This too can cause tension.

Such seeming inconsistencies have been stumbling blocks to many in the Christian community, producing denominationalism, cultism, and on a personal level, a struggle with application of God's Word. An example of this among the cults can be seen in the Jehovah's Witnesses' handling of the seeming contradiction between Christ's deity and His humanity. They simply deny His deity. The tension that many feel regarding heaven and hell is resolved by the Jehovah's Witnesses in their denial of hell. They simply erase the conflict by ignoring half the truth.

Although we cannot resolve all the debates concerning the conflicts of the Scriptures, we obviously cannot follow the cults' lead by eliminating half the truth. We must face the inconsistencies and realize that, first, there is no such thing as a nonessential commandment; and second, our focus should be on application rather than resolution. No command in Scripture calls us to resolve seeming contradictions. Rather, God calls us to apply and obey even when we do not fully understand.

3. *Ill-defined.* How can believers know where they stand in relationship to God? Some commandments are negative and others are positive. Negative commandments, such as the prohibitions against murder, adultery, stealing, and lying, are of such importance to God that He expects us to obey them in spite of our attitude. They are easily defined and measurable; each person knows whether he or she has broken these commandments. Not so with the positive commandments, such as "love thy neighbor" and "let the word of Christ dwell in you richly." The positive commandments deal primarily with attitudes. They strike at the very heart of a person's relationship with God. And they are not measurable. Therefore, believers have a hard time coming to grips with how to obey, simply because they are never quite certain where they stand in relation to the commands.

For example, if someone were to ask, "Do you love and honor your parents the way you ought?" you might answer the question hesitantly, stutter, and eventually ask, "Compared with what?" This is the problem with the positive commands. All good man-made laws are stated negatively. "Affirmative action" is a process of enacting positive laws, yet such laws seem to end in litigation, simply because they are unmeasurable and therefore, in a certain sense, relative. Committing ourselves to the positive commandments entails great risk.

Because the Bible appears to be illogical, inconsistent, and ill-defined, people hesitate to commit to what the Bible expects. While the process of commitment itself tends to remove the apprehension involved in risk taking and builds assurance, it can never eliminate the risk.

When I first began flying, I boarded the aircraft in fear and trepidation. Anxiety surged through my soul as the plane lifted off the ground, and my knuckles turned white as I grasped the side of the chair, trying to stabilize myself. With increased travel the fear subsided, and I became able to fall asleep while the plane was flying. Confidence was built, but risk was not eliminated.

The fear, or lack of it, was not the determining factor in the aircraft's safety.

BUILDING CONFIDENCE

Obeying God's commands appears to carry varying degrees of risk depending on one's place in the sanctification process. The more mature the person is, the less threatening the risks seem. Before coming to Christ, a person may fear commitment to the Savior because he or she thinks, "If I become a Christian, God may send me as a missionary to some foreign country." As one becomes a Christian and begins to mature in Christ, such apprehensions begin to fade. Nonetheless, the transformation that Scripture requires is so far-reaching that even the mature Christian quakes at the implications.

One of the most awesome illustrations of risk taking was when God asked Abraham to take Isaac to Mount Moriah and offer him as a sacrifice. How would God have communicated such a command to Abraham so that he would believe it? The command was for Abraham to take his son and kill him. In all probability, if God spoke to us in an audible voice, we would think we were hallucinating. If He wrote the message in the clouds, we would consider it a freak of nature. If He communicated through an angel, we would think it was the devil disguised as an angel of light. Furthermore, we would be hard pressed to find somebody who would concur with us when we went for counsel.

How, then, does one prepare for those frightful moments when God calls on us to do what appears to be nonsensical? How do we muster up enough faith to risk obedience to God?

There is no easy answer. Sensitivity, teachability, a willingness to die to self are all-important ingredients. But our confidence in the reasonableness of God's request is in direct proportion to the degree to which we have stepped out by faith and obeyed Him in the past. As far as we can tell from the biblical narrative, one of the first requests God made of Abraham was to leave Ur of the Chaldeans and embark "even though he did not know where he was going" (Hebrews 11:8). From the start, Abraham led a life of faith, insisting that his cultural grid conform to God's commandments rather than vice versa. It was his habit to obey God despite the implications, so that as God "upped the ante," so to speak, Abraham had experience from which to draw courage. As his confidence in God grew, his willingness to take even greater risks with God also grew.

PROCESS OR PRODUCT

When we are called on to walk by faith, we must remember that we usually tend to look at the *product*, whereas God always looks at the *process*. When God asked Abraham to take Isaac to Mount Moriah as a sacrifice, for example, Abraham was preoccupied with the question of what would happen to Isaac once he was killed. Would God, in fact, raise him from the dead? God knew the answer to that. What delighted God was that Abraham was willing to take the walk with Isaac to Mount Moriah. Abraham's focus was on the result; God's focus was on the process.

Elijah's confrontation with the prophets of Baal on Mount Carmel (1 Kings 18:17–46) affords another illustration. A contest arose between Baal, represented by his prophets, and the God of Israel, represented by Elijah. Baal's prophets were to offer a sacrifice, calling on their god to consume it with fire. Elijah was to follow in his turn. All through the day they called on Baal in vain. Knowing that the sacrifice would never be lit, Elijah mocked and derided them: "Maybe your god is deaf; maybe he's gone on vacation; maybe he's asleep; cry a little louder!"

Perhaps a certain amount of anxiety arose in Elijah during this drama. He had no doubt that they would never get their sacrifice consumed by fire from heaven; but would God light his? At the end of the day, when it was Elijah's turn, he had his sacrifice thoroughly soaked with water. Perhaps he engaged in a little theatrics knowing that if God was going to consume his sacrifice with fire, a bit of water would not hinder Him.

Elijah was preoccupied with the question, "Will God light my fire?" This was no issue with God; God knew how the episode would end. But Elijah's willingness to take the risk and step out by faith delighted God.

HOLINESS AND FAITH

Contrary to popular opinion, what pleases God is not a person's holiness, but a willingness to take risks commensurate with knowledge. The striking contrast between Rahab the harlot (Joshua 2) and the Scribes and Pharisees of Jesus' day illustrates this fact.

The Scriptures are blunt in pointing out Rahab's moral faults. She was a harlot, a liar, a cheat, willing to sell her own country into annihilation to save her skin. Although her lifestyle was not nearly as "righteous" as that of the Scribes and Pharisees, they received the scathing denunciation of God, while she has a place in the "Hall of Fame" (Hebrews 11:31). The Scribes and Pharisees knew a great deal, but they were short on application. Rahab knew very little, but she applied what she knew and took great risks in the process. A person delights God when he or she is willing to take the risks necessary to apply what God asks.

God is exceedingly gracious and patient as we take our painstaking steps on the road to sanctification. The Lord is less concerned with our position on the road than with our willingness to apply what we know. Belief in the Bible is always active, never passive. In Hebrews 11, faith and risk taking are always translated into action—committing before knowing, walking by faith.

PRINCIPLES FOR MEDITATION

4. Surrender is the cornerstone of all application. Refusal to surrender blurs our ability to discover and do God's will.
6. In those areas of life not addressed by the Scriptures, we must develop personal convictions to govern our behavior.
7. When applying the Scriptures, we must make a distinction between the positive and negative commandments.
8. Each person is individually responsible for applying the Scriptures to his or her own life.
9. In all things, we must be teachable. We must be willing to admit that we are wrong, change direction, and appear inconsistent.

QUESTIONS FOR DISCUSSION

1. In your own words, define "biblical faith."
2. Of all that God could ask of you, what would require the most faith? If God should ask, are you willing to do it?
3. Explain in your own words the correlation between biblical faith and the *process* of application.

6 Who In The World Is Meeting My Needs?

The famous psychologist Abraham Maslow theorized that humans have a hierarchy of needs. We have basic needs, he says, the most fundamental being our physical needs. The second is security, followed by love, self-acceptance, and self-actualization. Maslow's thesis is that these human needs must be met in ascending order: physical needs must be met before security; the need for security before love; love before self-acceptance; and self-acceptance before self-actualization. Although we may take exception with Maslow's order, all of us have needs—needs that are God-given and, therefore, legitimate. That being true, each individual must ask, "Who in the world is going to meet my needs?" In what direction is a person to look? A person has two basic choices: (1) To meet his or her own needs or (2) to allow God to meet those needs.

A PERSON IS RESPONSIBLE FOR MEETING HIS OR HER OWN NEEDS

Maslow's hierarchy is predicated on the assumption that each person is responsible for meeting his or her own needs. Not only do most non-Christians work from this assumption, but most Christians also live their lives assuming they must meet their own needs. Where does this assumption lead? What can we expect if we seek to meet our own needs?

1. *Our needs are insatiable and can never be met.* A person's needs are like a black hole in space; no matter how much time and energy are thrown into it, it consumes all and cries out for more.

We can sit down to a magnificent meal, for example, and literally stuff ourselves so that we leave the table feeling uncomfortable and insisting that we could not possibly eat another bite. Yet no matter how full we are, it is simply a matter of time before we are ready to eat again. No meal, no matter how satisfying, can do more than temporarily meet our desire for food.

What is true of food can be said for every other appetite—money, sex, power. Giving vent to the appetites causes us to look for newer and more exotic ways to meet them. Those appetites, however, can never be permanently satisfied.

2. *We use people to meet our needs.* Because our needs are insatiable we begin to look to sources outside ourselves to meet them. The cruel truth is that we use people to meet our needs.

After losing his wife to cancer, a friend of ours experienced a period of adjustment. He met a widow who had also lost her husband to cancer, and they began courting. They married and seemed to do well for a while. When they finally separated, the cause was apparent. Each compared the other with the former spouse. Because time tends to obliterate faults and accentuate strengths, as the new mate was compared with the former one, he or she was found wanting. They had entered into marriage to have their own needs met, and each used the other for that purpose. This example is a microcosm of modern society. The individual's needs are uppermost in all interpersonal relationships, and this self-centeredness breeds a lack of commitment. Faithlessness is found in sex without marriage and in divorce. It manifests itself in a lack of loyalty to one's family, employer, and country. It is at the heart of the "me" generation. It is the most grotesque form of selfishness, the antithesis of the biblical teaching that "it is more blessed to give than to receive."

3. *We compete with others.* Society teaches that our self-worth is wrapped up in our ability to compete with other people. In the academic world, worth is measured by one's grade-point average, being class validictorian, graduating *magna cum laude,* or becoming a Rhodes scholar. In athletics, value lies in beating one's opponent. An athlete is great to the degree that he is able to pulverize the opposition in the boxing ring, on the tennis court, or on the football field. In business, the successful person outsmarts the competitors by getting there first with the best and the most.

Competition within families is one of the most destructive expressions of this phenomenon. We have all listened to conversations in which the wife relates an episode, only to have her husband constantly correct her. "No, dear, it wasn't Tuesday; it was Wednesday"; "No, sweetheart, it wasn't at the hotel; it was at the motel"; "No, honey, it didn't happen in Dallas; it happened in Atlanta"; "No, dear, it wasn't the bellhop; it was the waiter." The husband who corrects his wife makes himself look smarter or wiser at the expense of his spouse.

Competition for challenge and enjoyment is biblically permis-

sible; competing for the fulfillment of one's need for personal
worth lies outside biblical limits. Nowhere in the ministry of our
Lord Jesus do we find any indication that He competed with
anyone. Such competition is a refutation of God's claim to be
able to meet the needs that exist in our lives.

4. *It is a denial of God's willingness to meet our needs.* The
Christian is frequently accused of using his faith in God as a
crutch. Of course God is our crutch! If we do not use God as a
crutch, we will ultimately use people as crutches, and nothing is
more grotesque or hideous.

The denial of God's willingness to meet needs was the issue
surrounding the expulsion of Adam and Eve from the Garden. In
essence, Satan said, "You have some needs that God is
unwilling to meet. You must take the initiative and meet them
yourselves. See that tree over there—the tree of the Knowledge
of Good and Evil? Take the initiative; assert yourself. After all,
God helps those who help themselves."

If we do not allow God to meet our needs, we will invariably
use people to meet them. Not only does this kind of exploitation
result in broken relationships, it also leads to breaking God's
commandments. Most of what we call the "horizontal commandments," which concern our relationship with others, were
written for this reason. God knew that we, in our independence,
would insist on looking to sources outside of Him to meet our
needs. Therefore, in the commandments He set limits to our
endeavor to do so.

God commands, "Thou shalt not steal." Why do people steal?
Obviously, it meets those needs that the thief perceives are not
being met. Again, He commands, "Thou shalt not commit
adultery." Why do people commit adultery? To meet their
unmet needs.

The summary of the Law, according to the Scriptures, is:
"Thou shalt love the Lord thy God with all thy heart, soul,
strength, and mind, and thy neighbor as thyself." No one can

begin to keep this summary of the Law while trying to meet his or her own needs!

LOOKING TO GOD TO MEET OUR NEEDS

Jesus, in His Sermon on the Mount, focuses our attention on God's desire to meet our needs:

> I tell you, do not worry about your life, what you will eat or drink; or about your body, what you will wear. Is not life more important than food, and the body more important than clothes? Look at the birds of the air; they do not sow or reap or store away in barns, and yet your heavenly Father feeds them. Are you not much more valuable than they? Who of you by worrying can add a single hour to his life?
>
> And why do you worry about clothes? See how the lilies of the field grow. They do not labor or spin. Yet I tell you that not even Solomon in all his splendor was dressed like one of these. If that is how God clothes the grass of the field, which is here today and tomorrow is thrown into the fire, will he not much more clothe you, O you of little faith? So do not worry, saying, "What shall we eat?" or "What shall we drink?" or "What shall we wear?" For the pagans run after all these things, and your heavenly Father knows that you need them. But seek first his kingdom and his righteousness, and all these things will be given to you as well. Therefore do not worry about tomorrow, for tomorrow will worry about itself. Each day has enough trouble of its own. (Matthew 6:25–34)

In Philippians 4:19 the apostle Paul reiterates: "My God will meet all your needs according to his glorious riches in Christ Jesus."

Both passages refer to physical needs, but the principle is applicable to all areas of life. To look to God to meet needs, however, we must accept two truths:

1. *God is sovereign and in total control.* When our eldest son was dying of leukemia, a friend wrote and said, "I believe that although God may have allowed it to happen, He certainly did not cause this disease to take your son's life. Your son's dying of leukemia is not the perfect will of God." I thought a great deal

about this statement and concluded that, if my son did not have leukemia by providential decree—if God did not cause it to happen—then He was out of control.

If God were not in control, then I have problems far greater than my son's cancer. Then God is in heaven, wringing His hands, hoping that things will turn out all right. When they aren't His perfect will, He is forced to rearrange things so that they ultimately work out for good.

The film *Heaven Can Wait* is the story of God out of control. An athlete dies before his time; his body is cremated before the forces of heaven can take charge; and then God must work things out for the man's good simply because God was not in control all the time.

Many are persuaded that Job suffered at Satan's hand, but the Bible teaches differently: "Then the LORD said to Satan, "Have you considered my servant Job? There is no one on earth like him; he is blameless and upright, a man who fears God and shuns evil. And he still maintains his integrity, though you incited me against him to ruin him without any reason" (Job 2:3).

God says that He destroyed Job—seemingly without cause. No fault or wrong precipitated the crisis through which he went. Even though Job did not understand what was taking place, there was purpose behind his tribulation.

2. *God has our best interests at heart.* At Kadesh-Barnea the spies of Israel were sent into the Promised Land, and they returned with an evil report. Because of Israel's unbelief, they wandered in the wilderness for forty years.

Commenting on this episode, the writer of Hebrews (chapter 3) says that God was testing Israel, and that Israel was testing God. In other words, God had Israel's best interests at heart, and Israel had Israel's best interests at heart. Both parties were agreed that Israel's welfare was uppermost. The conflict came when God said "facing the giants is in your best interest." Israel responded, "Facing the giants is not in our best interest."

Because the Israelites did not believe that God was concerned with their welfare, they wandered in the wilderness for the next forty years.

IMPLICATIONS OF YOUR CHOICE

If we do not believe that God is in control and has our best interests at heart, we can never look to Him to meet our needs. We will renege on any commitment and ultimately take charge in an effort to meet our own needs. The constant flow of circumstances through each person's life challenges those two basic convictions. A loved one dies of cancer; an automobile accident leaves me permanently injured; I commit my business to the Lord only to see it end in bankruptcy. These challenges confronted Job as he went "through the valley of the shadow of death." Was God really in control, and did He really have Job's best interests at heart? Even though the presence of his three friends caused him to go through spiritual vertigo, Job never yielded on these two points. He cried out in Job 13:15, "Though he slay me, yet will I hope in him."

If God is faithful, what are the implications for us? *We can never look to sources other than God to meet our needs.* We cannot look to spouse, children, church, friends, job, country. God, and God alone, is in the business of meeting needs, and He is jealous that we look solely to Him. The Psalmist expresses it this way: "Find rest, O my soul, in God alone; my hope comes from him" (Psalm 62:5).

This principle does not exclude God from using other people to meet needs in our lives; often He does. Our husbands, wives, children meet our needs in a marvelous way. Nevertheless, we cannot look to family, or any one other than God. If we do, we end up frustrated and jeopardizing relationships.

We relate to people in the same way that Jesus did when He said, "The Son of Man did not come to be served, but to serve, and to give his life . . ." (Mark 10:45). The Savior's ministry was marked by His willingness to give and give again.

As we enter into relationships, we can generally count on giving more than we receive. If we were honest, we would admit that in most relationships, whether with spouse, children, or friends, we feel we have given more to maintain that relationship than we have received from it. This perception is normal and natural, and thus we must look to God rather than to people to meet our needs.

THE SACRIFICE OF PRAISE

As he concludes his epistle, the writer of Hebrews gives an interesting challenge: "Through Jesus, therefore, let us continually offer to God a sacrifice of praise—the fruit of lips that confess his name" (Hebrews 13:15).

Praise is easy when things are going well. When, however, we feel our needs are not being met, giving praise is exceedingly difficult. To praise God during difficult moments, we must sacrifice at least two things:

1. *Our insatiable desire to know why.* Most of the time we address the question "why" to God when things are going badly. Rarely do we ask "why" when things are going well. Seldom do we hear someone say, "Why is God so good to me? Why did He bless and prosper my business? Why has He given us good health? Why hasn't our house burned down?"

We most frequently address the question to God when we feel that things are not going the way they ought. Sometimes "why" is a cry of anguish, as seen in the ministry of our Lord Jesus when He cried out on the cross, "My God, my God, why have you forsaken me?" (Matthew 27:46). Such a cry does not include an obsession for an answer.

There is another kind of "why," however—the persistent probing of God when things appear to be going badly. Such a question has at its root the desire to vote on the question of whether God in fact really has my best interest at heart. In essence, what I am saying is, "Okay, God, You said that You had my welfare at heart. There is no way in the world that I can conclude that these circumstances are in my best interest. Explain why You have allowed them to come into my life, and I'll vote on whether or not I agree with You.''

To praise God, we must sacrifice our desire to know why.

2. *The enjoyment of self-pity.* Humans find a perverse pleasure in feeling sorry for themselves. Wallowing in self-pity is an enjoyable experience, but it is difficult, if not impossible, to praise God while doing so.

CONCLUSION

None of us can live consistently. All of us backslide; all of us, no matter how firm our commitment to the contrary, regress into looking to others to meet our needs. To remedy this, we need to evaluate certain aspects of our trust in God:

1. *Foundation:* Do I really believe that God is sovereign, that He has my best interest at heart? Have I laid this foundation so that it is a non-negotiable conviction in life? Until I do, I can go no further. If I am not irrevocably committed to these truths, there is no way that I will be able to look to God to meet my needs.

2. *Awareness:* Am I aware that I tend to look to others to meet my needs? Two indicators of this tendency are the desire to know *why* and *self-pity.* Many people spin off in disappointment and self-pity, allow their relationship with God to be broken, and never really understand why. These two symptoms sound the alarm in our lives. Once we are aware of them, we must return to the cause and rectify the problem.

3. *Commitment:* Commitment is a sacred thing and must not be taken lightly. Since God would have us look to Him rather than others to meet our needs, we must covenant with Him to depend upon Him alone. We should commit ourselves before God never again, by His grace, to look to sources other than Him to meet our needs.

APPLICATION

Altering our filter system is foundational to change, but change is frightening, entailing great risk. The Christian who wants to see profound change in his or her life must look to God only for the meeting of needs. If we do not depend on God alone:

1. We will relegate application to a "do list," neglecting the more profound aspects of application, the mind's transformation.

2. The "do list" remains within the limits of our comfort and will be confined to such inane and innocuous activities as writing a letter to Aunt Sue, apologizing to Mr. Jones for being late, and "trying to be a better husband."

We can never take the risks entailed in application if we believe that we are responsible for meeting our own needs. If we do not believe that God is sovereign and has our best interests at heart, we will ultimately renege in whatever commitment we have made to God and, like the children of Israel at Kadesh-Barnea, evaluate God's commands in light of what we perceive is best for us. Changing one's filter, which results in transforming the mind, is a threatening renovation, for it challenges the very foundation of our being. If these truths are not firmly accepted, we will be unable to take the risks necessary to embark on the application process.

PRINCIPLES FOR MEDITATION

2. Every problem a person has is related to his or her concept of God.

10. The acknowledgment of wrong must be followed by restitution when it is within our power.

17. We must refuse to yield to what we know is wrong. Satisfying the drive will only momentarily alleviate the hunger and will stimulate a desire for more.

21. The validity of personal application is not dependent on another's acceptance or approval.

22. We must resist the temptation to judge others as less spiritual when they do what the Lord has forbidden us to do.

QUESTIONS FOR DISCUSSION

1. How would you answer a person who says, "Why does God want me to work at meeting the needs of others while at the same time looking only to Him to meet my needs?"
2. Identify a need in your life that you find difficult to trust God to meet. Why do you feel this way?
3. Explain in your own words the correlation between looking to God to meet your needs and the *process* of application.

7 Motivation

Jane has just finished a hard day at the office. When she returns to her apartment, she flops on the sofa and contemplates her weariness. Too tired to cook, she decides to skip dinner, take a hot bath, and go to bed early. Suddenly the phone rings. Sean, a young man in whom she has been interested, apologizes for the last-minute call and asks her out for dinner. Immediately filled with new energy, Jane eagerly prepares for her date.

Jane was unmotivated one moment, highly motivated the next. Can we encourage people to respond to the Scriptures the way Jane responded to Sean's call?

Motivation is important in the process of application. A person can understand the importance of application, learn how to apply

God's Word, but never grow because of improper motivation or lack of it. In light of the truths about risk taking, the demands of Scripture are so opposed to the world's perception that they can appear to be threatening, thereby reducing one's motivation to obey God's Word.

WHAT IS MOTIVATION?

Webster defines "to motivate" this way: "to impel, incite; to stimulate the active interest of." Industrial psychologists tell us that there are two components of motivation: The first is the *initiator*, that which gets a person started, the reason for action; the second is the *sustainer*, that which keeps a person on course without changing direction or abandoning purpose.

These two components, *initiating* and *sustaining*, are found in God's plan for motivation as well. Hebrews 11:6 says: "And without faith it is impossible to please God, because anyone who comes to him must believe that he exists and that he rewards those who earnestly seek him." This verse tells us that faith is essential to please God, that we must believe two things: *God is,* and *He rewards those who seek Him.* God has provided these two truths to motivate us.

Believers are motivated to apply the Scriptures because they have met God in the person of Jesus Christ. Through salvation we discover that *God is,* and we are consequently motivated to do what He says. From a biblical perspective, therefore, the *initiator* is God.

Believing that God "rewards those who seek him" is the second component, the *sustainer.* Throughout the Scriptures God has made certain promises to the believer, promises that sustain the believer and keep him or her on course to finish the race of life.

FAITH VS. HOPE

God's strategy for motivation begins with faith, and then it works toward hope. Hebrews 11:6 is part of the great chapter on faith. Faith is commitment before knowledge. What we put our faith in, the object of our faith, determines first, what we call it. If the object of our risk taking is God, we call it biblical faith.

The object of our faith determines its validity. Not how much faith we have but in what we put our faith determines whether that faith is valid. I can go to a physician with an illness, for example, and be fearful of the cure he prescribes. With great anxiety and apprehension I do it, only to find that he is correct. The next time I am ill, I go to a friend who is unqualified to diagnose or prescribe a remedy, but with a great deal of faith in him I follow his suggestion and become even more ill. This analogy demonstrates that it is not the amount of faith that I have that makes the difference, but who I put my faith in. The validity of the Christian's faith is found in its object—God.

Hebrews 11:1 specifies the correlation between faith and hope: "Now faith is being sure of what we hope for and certain of what we do not see." Faith is the pledge, assurance, or guarantee of things hoped for and the conviction of things not seen. The object of our faith is God. He has made us promises, as Hebrews 11 frequently reminds us. Accordingly, we believe these promises, because our hope is in God's character.

In other words, we commit ourselves (faith) in the direction of what our hope supports. If faith is risk taking, hope is why we take the risk again and again. In business, if I hope in what money will do for me, I will take my risks accordingly. As long as my hope is in the results that dollars can bring, I will persevere. Or I put my faith in the stock market, commodities, real estate, or some other venture, because my hope is in what the financial reward will be. To alter this course of trusting in money is to alter my hope.

In politics, if my hope is in the fame and recognition that public office affords, I will risk whatever is necessary to be elected. Because I hope for national recognition, I place my faith in the political system.

Jesus gives another illustration of this truth: "If you lend to those from whom you expect repayment, what credit is that to you? For 'sinners' lend to 'sinners,' expecting to be repaid in full" (Luke 6:34).

The hope of receiving motivates people to lend. Both benevolent giving and Christian giving are risk taking; the difference is the object of the faith. Jesus says that the world lends to receive an earthly reward. The Christian lends or gives to receive a heavenly reward. If I am motivated by the world's rewards, I will participate until my pain level tells me I should stop. If, however, I am motivated by my reward in heaven, I will give even to the point of poverty because of my hope in God's character. What I am hoping in makes the difference.

Hope, then, is the focus of motivation, but it must be properly placed. The Bible assures us that if our hope is focused on anything other than God's character, it will lead to despair. God's promises are an extension of God's character; I may wish for the promises, but my hope is always ultimately centered on God's character.

Hope lies in the object of our faith, and this in turn motivates us. Motivation has two major functions, initiating and sustaining—as seen in Hebrews 11:6: (1) God is, and (2) He rewards those who seek Him. Hope is only as valid as the object of our faith.

The story of Moses is a lesson in determining the object of faith. Moses understood the difference between hoping in the world's system and hoping in God's character. Hebrews 11:24–25 says: "By faith Moses, when he had grown up, refused to be known as the son of Pharaoh's daughter. He chose to be mistreated along with the people of God rather than to enjoy the pleasures of sin."

The hope that Moses exhibited in this decision sustained him over the years that followed, in his days in the wilderness and during his days of leading the Jewish nation. Moses is the epitome of a man who focused on the true hope of life, a hope centered on God's character.

A CLOSER LOOK AT HOPE

A high-school basketball team is practicing. The coach has the boys do an exercise that consists of a series of dashes interspersed with other exercises such as push-ups and sit-ups. On and on they go, straining every muscle in their young bodies. The pain is apparent on their faces as they try to keep up. Why are they doing this? What motivates them to maintain this pace and endure this pain? The answer is apparent: They hope to be on the starting team, to be winners. They hope for the applause and accolades of student body, faculty, and parents. They hope to gain acceptance from their peers. Such success, they reason, will make them happy, and this hope causes them to push beyond what they thought they could endure.

Hope is a powerful motivator. It is the truth a man will live and die for. Hope is man's projection of the future. Hebrews 11:24–26 notes that Moses expected God to reward him. Phillips translates it: "For he looked steadily at the ultimate, not the immediate, reward."

Hope is closely related to expectations. From a biblical perspective, positive expectations are always synonymous with hope; negative expectations are always synonymous with fear. The Bible holds no uncertainty, as does all else in life, regarding hope. Because of God's character, no doubts are ever cast on the fulfillment of biblical hope.

The Bible says we are *not* to hope in riches: "If I have put my trust in gold or said to pure gold, 'You are my security,' . . . these also would be sins to be judged, for I would have been unfaithful to God on high" (Job 31:24, 28).

Job, a godly man, knew he should not hope in the world's riches or circumstances, and he declared his hope: "Though he slay me, yet will I hope in Him" (Job 13:15).

God, speaking through Jeremiah, warns against trusting in people: "Cursed is the one who trusts in man, who depends on flesh for his strength and whose heart turns away from the LORD" (Jeremiah 17:5). Hope is inextricably linked to trust. God's people are not to trust in others.

Furthermore, sinners are warned not to trust in their own righteousness: "If I tell the righteous man that he will surely live, but then he trusts in his righteousness and does evil, none of the righteous things he has done will be remembered; he will die for the evil he has done" (Ezekiel 33:13).

If we have never sinned or transgressed God's commandments, we can place our hope in our own righteousness. But since "all have sinned and fall short of the glory of God" (Romans 3:23), trusting in our own righteousness is fatal.

Again, we are taught that we should not trust in a "dumb idol": "Of what value is an idol, since a man has carved it? Or an image that teaches lies? For he who makes it trusts in his own creation; he makes idols that cannot speak" (Habakkuk 2:18).

Habakkuk reminds us that idolatry is trusting in ourselves or anything that we make. At this point, secular motivation and Christian motivation separate. The former points to trusting in ourselves, a motivation based on our own character. Christian motivation, on the other hand, calls us to put our hope only in God's nature.

This contrast is seen in the nature of Old Testament Law: "There is perhaps no more striking proof of this thesis than in the fact that the schools of Hillel and Shammai disputed for more than two years whether it were better for man not to have been created or whether it is good for him to have been created, and that they finally agreed that it were better for him not to be created.''[1] Hillel and Shammai were Jewish leaders who meticulously followed the law, and concluded that the law produces despair. God's law only shows ourselves to ourselves.

Hope in anything other than the salvation provided by Jesus Christ produces despair. Because life and all that it holds is temporal, hope for the Christian must ultimately be in the eternal. Paul reminds the Corinthians of this in 2 Corinthians 4:16–18: "Therefore we do not lose heart. Though outwardly we are wasting away, yet inwardly we are being renewed day by day. For our light and momentary troubles are achieving for us an eternal glory that far outweighs them all. So we fix our eyes not on what is seen, but on what is unseen. For what is seen is temporary, but what is unseen is eternal."

Since the eternal is future, for those of us living in the temporal our hope is also in the future.

FOUR KINDS OF PEOPLE

In terms of hope, people can be divided into four categories:

1. *Those with no hope.* These people are most clearly illustrated by the philosophy of existentialism. The existentialist argues that life is meaningless. We don't know where we came from or where we are going. Therefore, the present is all-important. They call our era "The Now Generation." We didn't have yesterday, and we don't have tomorrow, all we have is now. Therefore, we seek to glean from now all we can get. The existentialist tends to be very experiential in his or her endeavor to live for now, whether through sex, drugs, or a long walk in nature.

Existentialism becomes a very selfish philosophy of life. Because there is no hope, people live to meet their own needs. Despair inevitably results; trusting only in one's own character always produces despair.

---

[1]G. Kittle, ed., *Theological Dictionary of the New Testament, Vol. 2* (Grand Rapids, Mich.: Eerdmans), 528.

2. *Those who have a misplaced hope.* How often we hear people answer the question, "Is it going to turn out all right?" with, "I hope so." The object of our faith determines the validity of our faith. Therefore, *if the object of our faith is any one other than God and our hope is in anything other than what He has promised, it is a misplaced hope.*

3. *Those who have an ill-defined hope.* Some Christians live like non-Christians. They have put their faith and trust in Jesus Christ, but they have put their hope in the world's value system. If asked if they were hoping in "uncertain riches," they would categorically deny it, but their lifestyles say otherwise. They are existing in spiritual schizophrenia; they have their faith in Jesus Christ's salvation but their hope in the world's value system.

They live in a confused and ill-defined state. Although they profess to know God, there is nothing in their lives that would lead people to believe that their hope is in God's promises. James describes such a person as "a wave of the sea, blown and tossed by the wind. . . . a double-minded man, unstable in all he does" (James 1:6, 8).

4. *Those who have a proper hope.* Hebrews 6:19 expresses such a hope: "We have this hope as an anchor for the soul, firm and secure. It enters the inner sanctuary behind the curtain."

Our hope, properly founded in God, is an anchor of the soul because our value system is shaped by hope that rests in God's character. Such hope gives stability because it causes all of life's decisions to be based on God's promises. A person's life will be the product of his or her hope. A person who places hope in Jesus Christ, the anchor of the soul, gains stability and direction.

Hope is a truth for which a person will live and die, that truth on which the person bases his or her entire life. The quality of the *object* of hope is important. Therein lies the distinction in the Christian life: we place our hope in the irrefutable power of God's character.

THE POWER OF HOPE

The apostle Peter understood that the product of one's life will be a direct result of one's hope: "But in your hearts set apart Christ as Lord. Always be prepared to give an answer to everyone who asks you to give the reason for the hope that you have. But do this with gentleness and respect" (1 Peter 3:15). This exhortation to holy living was given in the midst of persecution and opposition. If we by faith put into practice Scripture's admonitions and suffer for it, Peter says, others will ask for the reason for the hope that is in us. Believers take the risk of godly living, knowing that they will suffer for it, because their hope is in God's character.

1 John 3:3 says: "Everyone who has this hope in him purifies himself, just as he is pure." John indicates that hope produces purity of life, a distinctive trait in the believer's lifestyle. Such a lifestyle will be so powerful that the world will ask for an explanation. "Be ready for such an occasion," Peter admonishes.

The most frequent Old Testament illustration of a man who delights God because of his hope is Abraham: "Against all hope, Abraham in hope believed and so became the father of many nations, just as it had been said to him, 'So shall your offspring be.' Without weakening in his faith, he faced the fact that his body was as good as dead—since he was about a hundred years old—and that Sarah's womb was also dead. Yet he did not waver through unbelief regarding the promise of God, but was strengthened in his faith and gave glory to God, being fully persuaded that God had power to do what he had promised. This is why 'it was credited to him as righteousness'" (Romans 4:18–22).

God had promised Abraham and Sarah a son, but Abraham was about a hundred years old, and Sarah was no longer capable of childbearing. This couple had two choices: They could either

look at the facts, which indicated that they would never have a
son of their own, or they could look at God's promises. Verse 18
says that Abraham "against all hope" believed in hope that he
might become the father of many nations. He refused to trust in
the facts as the world saw them and placed his trust in God's
promises.

As people look at our lives, can they see that our hope is in
God's promises because of His character? Do they see us
applying the Scriptures, taking great risks in the process? Are we
being "conformed to the world," or are we being "transformed
by the renewing of our minds"? If we are motivated in the
direction of our hope, how do we answer when called on to
explain the hope that is governing our lives?

IDENTIFYING ONE'S HOPE

If we are unable to determine our hope, how do we go about
bringing it into focus? The apostle Paul in his letter to the
Romans gives a suggestion: "We also rejoice in our sufferings,
because we know that suffering produces perseverance; perseverance, character; and character, hope. And hope does not
disappoint us, because God has poured out his love into our
hearts by the Holy Spirit, whom he has given us" (Romans
5:3–5).

We can have a joyful attitude during times of suffering and
affliction because these tribulations produce (that is, fashion or
work out) perseverance, or patience. The application of Scripture, which is godly action in an ungodly world, may produce
tribulation; tribulation, in turn, requires perseverance. Perseverance implies that one has an opportunity to change circumstances but elects not to. If I have an automobile accident,
become a quadriplegic, and learn to live with it, for example, I
am not truly persevering in the biblical sense, because I can do
nothing to change my circumstances. True perseverance implies
that I can walk away from the tribulation but choose not to. I

persevere not because I have no choice, but because I elect to stay in the battle. I would rather apply God's Word than eliminate the suffering that such application produces.

Such perseverance, according to verse 4, will fashion proven character or experience—the Greek word *dokime*. *Dokime* means "an object which is tested to prove its genuine value; certified; tested and proved worthy." This testing to prove the genuineness of our character verifies the validity of the hope. The process is cyclical. Hope and God's promises cause us to persevere in the face of tribulation; this perseverance in turn proves the validity of our hope and causes us to long for the fulfillment of that hope.

As Paul develops his argument in Romans 5:5–11, he specifies two reasons why this hope will not disappoint us. First, the Holy Spirit assures our hearts that we are heading in the right direction. Second, when we were non-Christians and God's enemies, He took the initiative and died for us in the person of Christ. Now that we are His children in Christ, we are assured that these tribulations are not the product of His wrath but work for our good because of God's character. Our hope is not misplaced.

Most people try to evaluate their hope during good times. Often a sense of well-being causes a person to lose his or her sense of dependence on God. Paul teaches that our hope is tested and best understood during times of tribulation and perseverance.

Tribulation helps us to work out and clarify our hope. What do we cling to at the point of our deepest need? In his darkest hour, Job cried, "Though he slay me, yet will I hope in him" (Job 13:15).

Tribulation also helps to fashion our hope. Hope fashioned during times of stress and tribulation produces gentleness and empathy. Our hope is more clearly understood and embraced because we understand and "prove" God's character. Hope developed during good times is an untested hope and, consequently, tends to be unreliable.

James says: "Consider it pure joy, my brothers, whenever you face trials of many kinds, because you know that the testing of your faith develops perseverance. Perseverance must finish its work so that you may be mature and complete, not lacking anything" (James 1:2–4).

God states that the product of this endurance is that we may be made mature, not lacking anything. Not only do we endure because we *have* hope, the process of enduring *builds* hope!

As humans we are extremely vulnerable. If we are honest, we know that we are never far from an experience like Job's. Such suffering and hardship will reveal if our hope is improperly placed.

Scott, a successful executive on the west coast, has all the trappings of worldly success. He has climbed the corporate ladder, lives in a beautiful home in the suburbs, has an attractive wife and family, and is an active participant in his local church. Over the past twenty years, finances have never been a problem. His friends and associates know where he stands in his commitment to the church and to God, and he has demonstrated his faith by being generous with the resources God has given him.

Several years ago significant conflicts began to develop in the three major areas of his life—his family, his job, and his church. His commitment to the church had outstripped his commitment to the family, and that, his wife declared, had to change. Her second ultimatum had to do with his job: Scott's restlessness with his job, which had ceased to be fulfilling, had to be dealt with. When we met Scott, he readily confessed that major areas of his life had been burned away, and all he had left was ashes. His hopes were not coming to fruition.

Scott had hoped in money, planning to out-earn his needs and keep the family satisfied. He hoped that the position he had with

the corporation would give him self-worth. He hoped that by
hard work in the church he would meet God's expectations. In
short, he had placed his hope in God for salvation, but hoped in
the world for fulfillment and self-worth.

When we asked his purpose for existence, Scott was visibly
embarrassed and shaken because it was an issue he had never
seriously considered. He had a vague notion that he did not want
to give his life to "wood, hay and stubble," but as he began to
consider the direction of his life, he discovered that was exactly
what his life was producing. When Scott considered 1 Peter
3:15, evaluating how his family, friends, and associates would
view his hope, he began to realize that he had embraced a hope
that was contrary to his theology. He had leaned his ladder
against the wrong building. The contradiction of his hoping in
God for salvation but not for the totality of his life came into
focus, and he responded, "I am a totally carnal man."

Scott's tribulation forced him to realize that he had substituted
money, power, and position for biblical hope as the source of his
motivation. His tribulation forced him to recognize his error. In
the life of the believer, tribulation eliminates the alternatives to
biblical hope and brings into focus the truth that God alone is our
source. Like the drowning man who gasps, "God help me," the
understanding of hope is the elimination of alternatives. Our
hope, clarified during days of tribulation, becomes the anchor of
our souls in day-to-day living.

SUMMARY

Hope is the motivating force of life. All of us are motivated in
the direction of our hope, and those who have no hope are
unmotivated. Believers are motivated to obey the Scriptures
because their hope is in God's character. A clear understanding
of this hope gives boldness in taking steps that produce
Christlikeness in our lives.

When we apply the Scriptures and begin to develop Christlikeness in the face of tribulation, opposition, and persecution, the world will call on us to explain the object of our hope.

Since hope is necessary for motivation, biblical hope is necessary for application. If we are not applying the Scriptures, we either have no hope, a misplaced hope, or an ill-defined hope. Analyzing and defining our hope is an essential component to the application process.

PRINCIPLES FOR MEDITATION

2. Every problem a person has is related to his or her concept of God.
4. Surrender is the cornerstone of all application. Refusal to surrender blurs our ability to discover and do God's will.

QUESTIONS FOR DISCUSSION

1. Define ''hope'' in your own words, showing the distinction between faith and hope.
2. On pages 105–106 we analyzed four ways to hope. How do you hope? Why did you come to this conclusion?
3. Explain in your own words the correlation between having a proper hope and the *process* of application.

8 The Motive of Application

Most of us are reluctant to examine motives. Most Christians would confess that they have a hard time discovering their true motives, and what they do understand tends to be muddled and impure. In all honesty, we have probably never had a perfectly pure motive in all our lives.

The motivation for obedience is our hope in God's promises. That differs from motive in that we are *motivated* by God's promises, while our *motive* is the reward that the promises offer.

GOD MEETS US WHERE WE ARE

The Lord understands that everyone is motivated by personal gain. God's grace simply means that He meets us where we are and takes us to where we ought to be.

In the opening chapters of Job, God and Satan are talking, and the Lord draws Satan's attention to Job: "Have you considered my servant Job? There is no one on the earth like him; he is blameless and upright, a man who fears God and shuns evil" (Job 1:8).

Satan responds: "Does Job fear God for nothing? . . . Have you not put a hedge around him and his household and everything he has? You have blessed the work of his hands, so that his flocks and herds are spread throughout the land. But stretch out your hand and strike everything he has, and he will surely curse you to your face" (Job 1:9–11).

The Lord accepts Satan's challenge, allowing the devil to attack Job to test Job's motive for serving Him. In essence Satan said, "Honesty is the best policy. When it ceases to be the best policy, people cease to be honest."

Satan was expounding the philosophy of the person outside of Christ. The Lord's rebuttal is that although this may reflect the thinking of the unregenerate, when a person comes to Christ, his or her focus changes. Job did not serve God to prosper but because of the relationship between himself and God and because of the promise of that relationship in eternity. Job proves the point.

Even for Job, however, the issue was not a lack of desire for personal gain but where he hoped to find that gain. Although Job was a wealthy man, because of his relationship with God there was a transfer of his hope from this life to the future life. Thus, even in his despair he cried out: "I know that my Redeemer lives, and that in the end He will stand upon the earth. And after my skin has been destroyed, yet in my flesh I will see God; I myself will see him with my own eyes—I, and not another. How my heart yearns within me!" (Job 19:25–27).

Job understood that mortality is certain and that life on earth is brief. He hoped in God rather than in what this world had to offer even though he had acquired a great deal of this world's goods.

The debate between Satan and God over Job is a microcosm of the philosophy behind the process of evangelism. God has designed the gospel in such a way that it meets a person at a point of need—specifically, personal gain. In salvation a person trades death for life; hell for heaven; condemnation for commendation; the frustrated, empty life for the abundant life; alienation from God for favor with God. In short, we become Christians because, from a human perspective, "it is the best policy." Those who are able to see things clearly understand that a person cannot afford not to become a Christian. The more we recognize our wretched condition, the more attractive the gospel appears. The motive of the gospel is personal gain.

UNDERSTANDING GRACE

Salvation is a gift of God, dependent not on man's performance but on God's performance on man's behalf. The foundation of our salvation is the finished work of Christ, not our willingness to obey Him and certainly not our ability to live a holy life. The believer's relationship with God is secure "not because of righteous things we had done" (Titus 3:5) but by what Jesus did for us through His death on the cross.

Grace is unique to the Christian religion. In all other religions, a person's relationship with God is dependent on his performance. Only in Christianity is there no reciprocity. Only in Christianity does a person not have to worry about his or her relationship with God being jeopardized by performance.

Only in the Judeo-Christian tradition is the concept of grace introduced at all; it is not found anywhere else. Even for the mature believer grace can go out of focus. Nothing in human experience, apart from our relationship with God, helps us to understand grace. We knew something of faith before coming to Christ—an imperfect knowledge, perhaps, but everybody lives by some kind of faith.

People outside of Christ know something of love, albeit

imperfectly, for people love their spouses, their children, and their parents. And most people at one time or another have, in an act of mercy, withheld judgment.

But grace is absolutely unique to what God has offered in Christ Jesus, and maintaining a clear perspective on it is difficult. God says that all people must "commit before knowing," exercise faith, take risks. God's commitment, however, is based on perfect knowledge. His knowledge of us is so complete that we can never surprise Him. Many times we disappoint Him, but we never surprise Him. His acceptance of us will never be any greater or less than it is right now.

Paul, in his letter to the Romans, commands: "Therefore do not let sin reign in your mortal body so that you obey its evil desires. Do not offer the parts of your body to sin, as instruments of wickedness, but rather offer yourselves to God, as those who have been brought from death to life; and offer the parts of your body to him as instruments of righteousness" (Romans 6:12–13).

His rationale is found in verse 14: "For sin shall not be your master, because you are not under the law, but under grace." Here, as well as elsewhere in the Bible, obedience to the command is not a condition for salvation. God commands the believer to live an obedient life, but grace means that sin does not jeopardize a person's relationship with God.

LAW OF THE HARVEST

Some will no doubt argue that such liberty leads to license. If the believer's relationship with God is based on grace rather than obedience, why obey? What incentive, if any, is there for personal holiness? The answer is *rewards*.

Paul, writing to the churches in Galatia, said: "Do not be deceived: God cannot be mocked. A man reaps what he sows" (Galatians 6:7). This verse is traditionally called "The Law of the Harvest"—what a person sows, he or she reaps.

A person who understands security in Christ may feel that God is backed into a corner. That person can sin with impunity, knowing that God's commitment is based on the finished work of Christ rather than on that person's ability to live a holy life. He or she rationalizes, "I'll go ahead and sin, feel sorry for it afterward, and then confess, knowing that God will forgive me."

The principle may be true, but that person has forgotten the irrevocable consequences of sin: What a person sows, he or she reaps.

After several years of marriage and four children, Ted and Phyllis divorced. They have both subsequently remarried, but the scars are still evident. Ted says, "Eleven years after the divorce, my children are still split between two families. Because their mother and I have differing value systems, I am constantly having what I teach them challenged by their mother."

The irrevocable consequences of sin do not contradict God's willingness to forgive or His ability to forget. Once sin is set in motion, however, it follows its course to completion. All sins, whether in thought or in action, have irrevocable consequences. These consequences may not be felt in this life. When and how these consequences come to bear on the offender will vary, but Scripture's promise is that a person will reap what he or she sows.

SALVATION OR REWARD

A distinction must be maintained between salvation and reward. Salvation is based on what God does for me through Jesus Christ. Reward is based on what I do in response to what God has done for me. Salvation is based on God's performance; reward is based on my performance. Salvation affects the eternal destiny of the person. Reward affects the quality of that destiny either for good or for bad. Salvation is of grace; reward is of works.

Salvation and reward are the motives of obedience. Christians seek to please God out of gratitude for His gracious salvation.

They also apply the Word of God because they know that their reward in heaven will be affected by their obedience. The higher of these two motives seems to be gratitude for so great a salvation. As we read through the Scriptures, however, we find far more emphasis on reward as the motive for obedience than gratitude to God for His salvation.

These two facets are demonstrated in the ministry of the apostle Paul. In 2 Corinthians 5:14 he says, "Christ's love compels us." In 1 Corinthians 9:24–27 he says: "Do you not know that in a race all the runners run, but only one gets the prize? Run in such a way as to get the prize. Everyone who competes in the games goes into strict training. They do it to get a crown that will not last; but we do it to get a crown that will last forever. Therefore I do not run like a man running aimlessly; I do not fight like a man beating the air. No, I beat my body and make it my slave so that after I have preached to others, I myself will not be disqualified for the prize."

Obedience affects reward, but it does not affect salvation. Paul makes this clear: "If any man builds on this foundation using gold, silver, costly stones, wood, hay or straw, his work will be shown for what it is, because the Day will bring it to light. It will be revealed with fire, and the fire will test the quality of each man's work. If what he has built survives, he will receive his reward. If it is burned up, he will suffer loss; he himself will be saved, but only as one escaping through the flames" (1 Corinthians 3:12–15).

The quality of one's reward in heaven depends on whether that person has invested in "gold, silver, costly stones" or "wood, hay and straw." But if heaven is to be a place where there is no more crying and pain (Revelation 21:4), then how do the rewards differ? In what way is the quality of heaven different for the person who has invested in "gold, silver, costly stones" from that of the person who has invested in "wood, hay and straw"? The Bible is silent on this subject. The exact difference that our reward makes in heaven is unclear, but that it does make a difference is abundantly clear from the Scriptures on the subject (2 Corinthians 5:10–11).

Death is not a time of transformation but a time of confirmation. The Bible teaches that transformation only takes place in an encounter with Jesus Christ. When a person dies, he or she is simply confirmed in what is already done. In the last chapter of the last book in the Bible, John says: "Then he told me, 'Do not seal up the words of the prophecy of this book, because the time is near. Let him who does wrong continue to do wrong; let him who is vile continue to be vile; let him who does right continue to do right; and let him who is holy continue to be holy.'

" 'Behold, I am coming soon! My reward is with me, and I will give to everyone according to what he has done' " (Revelation 22:10–12).

The Bible is unclear as to the specific implications, but it is clear that people bring into eternity the essence of what they are. When a person slips into God's presence, he or she takes the ingredients that make up the real person. What we do in the few years that God gives us here on earth appreciably affects how we spend eternity.

THE BASIS OF REWARD

The parables of Jesus include three issues that might be considered regarding rewards:

1. *The amount of time invested.* In Matthew 20:1–16, the Parable of the Vineyard, people are invited to enter the vineyard at various times of the day, and at the end of their labor all are given the same reward. Because the believer's opportunity to participate in God's work and the length of time that person is there are expressions of God's grace, payment and reward are not based on the amount of time spent.

2. *The ability of the person making the investment.* In Matthew

25:14–30, in the Parable of the Talents, the master delivers to one servant five talents, to another two, and to another, one. Jesus demonstrates that people are gifted differently and have different responsibilities. In verses 21 and 23, the five-talented person receives the same reward as the two-talented person. Reward or payment is not given according to one's ability.

3. *The faithfulness of the person making the investment.* In Luke 19:11–24, in the Parable of the Ten Minas, the good master gives to each person the same amount, which indicates equal opportunity. Reward in the parable is based on faithfulness to opportunity.

The three parables indicate that reward is not based on the amount of time we serve God in the life we have here on earth; nor is it based on the abilities or talents that we have, since these are gifts from God. As demonstrated by the contrast between Rahab the harlot and and the Scribes and Pharisees of Jesus' day, it is based on faithfulness to the opportunities that God gives us. The walk of faith is based on taking risks, acting on what we know to be right; and obedience in turn produces holiness. But God is not pleased with how holy a person is, but with how holy he or she is in proportion to how much he or she knows. What delights God, and what becomes the basis or reward, is how faithful the person has been with the opportunities that God has given.

A QUESTION OF MOTIVES

We often assume that a pure motive implies an unselfish love that is bent on giving rather than receiving with no thought of personal gain. Certainly, the Bible calls on us to give sacrificially. Writing to the Philippians, Paul says: "Do nothing out of selfish ambition or vain conceit, but in humility consider others better than yourselves. Each of you should look not only to your own interests, but also to the interests of others" (Philippians 2:3–4).

Such unselfishness, however, does not mean that there is no thought of receiving gain. *Nowhere in the Bible are we taught that the motive of personal gain is wrong.* People err not in seeking personal gain but in how they go about seeking it. The Bible teaches that there is nothing wrong with wanting to get, live, lead, or be first. All are worthy and noble goals.

God merely insists that we go about obtaining them the right way. The secret to getting is giving; the key to living is dying; if we want to lead, we must be servants; if we want to be first, the way to accomplish it is by being last. The motive of reward is not wrong. Wrong only occurs when we do it our way rather than God's way.

Reward is a proper motive for obedience. Believers are never criticized or condemned for making reward a motive for obedience. In fact, the opposite seems to be the case. Jesus' words in Luke 6:35–38 combine good deeds with the desire for personal gain. And Jesus combines reward with personal sacrifice in His call to discipleship: "Peter answered him, 'We have left everything to follow you! What then will there be for us?'

"Jesus said to them, 'I tell you the truth, at the renewal of all things, when the Son of Man sits on his glorious throne, you who have followed me will also sit on twelve thrones, judging the twelve tribes of Israel. And everyone who has left houses or brothers or sisters or father or mother or children or fields for my sake will receive a hundred times as much and will inherit eternal life' " (Matthew 19:27–29).

All commands of self-sacrifice are made at no ultimate cost to self. God *always* says He will make it up to us. If we rebut with the argument that reward is not a pure motive, we set a standard higher than God's. The Bible does not recognize disinterested piety!

The certainty of accountability to God is an important motive in the application process. Jeremiah reveals the condition of the human heart when he says: "The heart is deceitful above all things and beyond cure. Who can understand it?'' (Jeremiah 17:9).

Without the promises of judgment and rewards, we would consider God's commandments negotiable. When all is going well, we are quick to affirm the importance and validity of the biblical commands, but when circumstances appear adverse, we are prone to take exception to what God says. At such times we are tempted to compromise the Scriptures for the sake of expedience. The "Law of the Harvest" is a powerful deterrent.

A QUESTION OF FOCUS

The focus of the Christian life must not be on holiness but on obedience. Holiness is the product or the standard; obedience is the process. When holiness becomes the focus, we begin to compare ourselves with others and in the process become Pharisaical. The Pharisees focused on holiness and thought that they could manipulate obedience.

If we focus on the product of holiness, we stop looking to God for the reward and begin to look to people for recognition. We develop comparative standards with others that logically leads us to establish a standard different from God's. Focusing on the product eliminates the risk, causing us to alter the standard to insure success.

Tithing, for example, is an Old Testament law which was done away with at the cross. The tithe required ten percent. If I focus on the product of ten percent in my giving program, certain results occur:

1. I eliminate the need to walk by faith. The Bible teaches that all that I have belongs to God. If I give ten percent with the attitude that the ninety percent belongs to me, I eliminate the need to trust God for deciding how much I should give. I may be trusting God for all that I get, but I cease trusting Him for what I give.

2. If I decide to give twenty percent, or twice the tithe, twice

the perceived standard, now I really look good. I may consider myself to be quite spiritual—maybe even holy. But if I were willing to take the risk of personal application, I might find that God wants me to give forty percent or fifty percent rather than just twenty percent. God is the standard.

3. Because my focus is on the product, if I give twenty percent, I compare myself favorably with the person who is giving only two percent. I look down on such a person, feeling that he is not very spiritual. In fact, however, he may be more spiritual than I, for in the application process he may be taking a greater risk in giving two percent than I am in giving twenty percent.

We find that God is not pleased with our holiness in comparison with others. Rather, He is pleased with our willingness to take the risks of obedience. If I focus on the process, I take the risk of obedience, lose my tendency to compare myself with others, realize that I cannot measure my holiness, and in the process become a delight to God. Paul, as he instructs the Corinthians on giving (2 Corinthians 9), deals with the attitude of giving, not with a formula for giving.

Misplaced piety focuses on holiness and calls people to a motive not demanded in the Scriptures, risking the possibility of missing God's standard. Holiness is not wrong, of course, but when we make it the objective, we tend to lose focus on the process. God calls all of us to a life of obedience. What that obedience looks like depends on where we are in the sanctification process. Our willingness to take the risks of altering our filter system and acting on what God says must be the emphasis of our lives. From a biblical perspective, reward is a legitimate motive in this process of obedience and cannot be overlooked in considering the issues of eternity.

PRINCIPLES FOR MEDITATION

11. We must consider God's command rather than His chastisement as the motive for application.

14. Although there is no distinction between sins, there is a difference in consequences.
15. Disobedience adds to confusion when adverse circumstances come.
24. Our conduct, good or bad, will affect the generations to follow.
25. We must maintain an accountability relationship with a group of people who will exhort us to faith and good works.

QUESTIONS FOR DISCUSSION

1. How do you feel about the motive of *reward* tied to being motivated to obey God? Does this seem radical or normal? Why?
2. Verbalize in your own words the difference between the biblical ideal of salvation and rewards.
3. Discuss the dangers in focusing on holiness or a person's good works in life rather than obedience.
4. Explain in your own words the correlation between being motivated by personal gain and the application process.

# The Source of Application

If we intend to engage in the application process, we must understand the source. If we are going to seek to do right, from what quarter is it going to be communicated to us? Obviously, the prime source of application for the Christian is the Bible, but there are also five other sources of application: authority, counsel, challenge, circumstances, and the Holy Spirit.

OBEDIENCE TO AN AUTHORITY

Peter admonishes: "Submit yourself for the Lord's sake to every authority instituted among men" (1 Peter 2:13), and Paul gives essentially the same command in Romans 13. This authority can come from a parent, teacher, police officer, employer, or such "laws of the land" as the speed limits.

This principle naturally raises questions concerning authority—that is, what is legitimate and what is illegitimate authority? This complex subject demands attention in an increasingly anti-authoritarian age.

In the New Testament some passages on authority refer to the submitter and some to the leader or ruler. God places His people under the authority of others. The believer is to submit to human authority "as unto the Lord," believing by faith that this authority is God-ordained. In the final analysis, submission is an issue of faith, not an evaluation of human leadership. From God's point of view the question of authority is between the believer and God, not the believer and the authority figure.

The leader, of course, is not absolved of responsibility. Quite the contrary. Because we tend to judge right and wrong through the cultural filter rather than through the biblical filter, average believers are more sensitive and amenable to human authority than they are to the Bible. Human authority not only makes rules but also couples with them the pressure of acceptance or rejection. This tendency produced the Pharisees in Israel and continues to produce Pharisees in today's churches.

Those in authority have a responsibility to test the rules and regulations that they make in light of biblical teaching. James cautions: "Let not many of you become teachers, my brethren, for you know that we who teach shall be judged with greater strictness" (James 3:1 RSV).

For all believers, the Scriptures are the final court of appeal. As the leaders of the Protestant Reformation stated, the Scriptures are "our only rule of faith and practice." When any authority, whether parent, church, or state, demands that the believer transgress one of the negative commandments, that authority must be respectfully disobeyed. If a parent tells the child to steal, murder, or lie, for example, the child is to obey God rather than man.

The two broad categories of human authority are the church and all other legitimate seats of authority.

The church belongs to Christ, not to man; therefore it stands as a category by itself. The church can only require the believer to do what the Bible commands. It cannot exact any standard of performance for the believer beyond biblical imperatives.

If my church says, for example, that I can only have two children, must live in a home no larger than three bedrooms, and can only drive one automobile, what should my response be? Does the church have the right to make such demands?

Let's answer the question this way: If a person is part of the Church of Jesus Christ but cannot belong to our church because of additional requirements we have imposed on him, we make "our church" a sect, because we have established conditions for membership different than Christ's. If the church belongs to Christ, then Christ and Christ alone can establish the requirements for membership.

All other authority figures are free to make demands on a person providing they do not transgress the negative commandments of Scripture: An employer can establish a thirty-minute lunch break; the teacher can insist that class begin at 8 A.M.; the state can insist that its citizens pay tax.

A distinction of course, must be maintained between voluntary and involuntary submission to authority. For example, a person's submission to his employer is voluntary; that is, if he does not like the rules and regulations laid down by the corporation, he can quit and work somewhere else. The rules and regulations of the state, however, are involuntary. The citizen is required to obey them and is penalized if he fails to do so.

Involuntary submission to authority, however, does not mean that authority is always obeyed. Even when the penalty is stiff, a person may thwart such authority, because most authority is delegated. The mother with an eighteen-year-old son knows that whatever authority she has over him is conferred to her by him. She may make him sorry if he fails to obey, but if he elects not to obey, there is nothing she can do.

The Scriptures clearly indicate that there are authorities ordained by God which should be a source of input into the believer's life. Their area of input is defined by biblical imperatives and cannot violate those imperatives. Because authority is delegated, we must remember that the issue is not the quality of leadership being given, but rather our willingness to accept that authority. With the proper attitude of submission, God can use these authorities to teach us a great deal and put us in a position where significant spiritual growth and application can take place.

COUNSEL

Solomon says: "The purposes of a man's heart are deep waters, but a man of understanding draws them out" (Proverbs 20:5). People of "understanding" will go to those who are wise or proficient in their respective fields for counsel. Such counsel is not necessarily binding, but it certainly becomes a source for action as the counselee evaluates the advice.

Again Solomon says: "Plans fail for lack of counsel, but with many advisers they succeed" (Proverbs 15:22). Clearly God wants us to use counsel as we seek to apply the Scriptures. Counsel should be used for two purposes: (1) to check the validity of our thinking, and (2) to obtain new or additional insights.

Although we tend to use counselors to make decisions for us, the Christian is ultimately accountable to God for his or her decisions. The counselor can never usurp that accountability, but godly counsel can help us to sort through our thinking and make sure that we have not overlooked important data.

God has given us wise and gifted people to help us in our sojourn. Although we are not obliged to follow their advice, we are certainly wise if we listen carefully to what they say. In following their advice, however, the decision is always ours. And as in the case of authority, the advice and counsel must be weighed in light of scriptural teachings.

THE THOUGHTS AND CHALLENGES OF OTHERS

The thoughts and challenges of others may come in the form of rebuke or exhortation and may not necessarily be the product of our requesting help. Such challenges are often offered to us in a spontaneous form as we go through life, coming from an enemy, a child, a friend, a television program, or a host of other sources. Perhaps I am working too hard, not spending adequate time with my family, allowing my health to degenerate. A friend comes with an exhortation for me to take better care of myself. I pray about it, reflect on it, and conclude that my friend is right. As a result, I take corrective measures.

Or perhaps I have been watching a television program that relates an episode of a man who began to live beyond his means. He develops a lifestyle and expectations that are impossible for him to maintain. As the pressure builds, he is tempted to step outside of the law and enter into some illegal enterprises. The program concludes with his being caught and sentenced to prison. As I reflect on the episode, I vow to avoid deficit spending and to live within my means.

The thoughts and challenges of other people, evaluated in light of what the Bible teaches, can be an important source of application for the teachable Christian.

CIRCUMSTANCES

God in His providence allows circumstances to flow through our lives. Viewed as either positive or negative, circumstances can heighten our awareness of the need for application.

People tend to consider circumstances important in determining whether God approves or disapproves of a particular course of action. Circumstances become the litmus paper of our relationship with Him. If we do right and gain God's approval, we reason, "God's blessing" will result. But when circumstances not to our liking enter our lives, we conclude that either

God is mad at us and we therefore must search our lives for what we have done wrong, or God does not really love us or have our best interests at heart.

The Bible teaches, however, that the "good guys" do not always win and the "bad guys" do not always lose. In Psalm 73, for example, the psalmist says, "But as for me, my feet had almost slipped; I had nearly lost my foothold. For I envied the arrogant when I saw the prosperity of the wicked" (Psalm 73:2–3). Those who do not serve God, he goes on to say, seem to be free from ills and burdens, while the righteous suffer.

The psalmist concludes that the fate of the wicked is desolation and destruction, but often their "reward" comes in the hereafter, not here on earth. Because the believer on earth is being prepared for eternity, God allows circumstances to enter his or her life that appear tragic. Such was the case with Job, whom God Himself ruined without any reason (Job 2:3).

Circumstances can heighten our awareness of the need for application, though care must be taken as we evaluate those circumstances. *When the devil accuses, he does it in generalities.* Vague feelings of sin, unworthiness, doubt, and insecurity are not the product of the Holy Spirit. *When the Holy Spirit convicts, He does it in specifics.* The Christian's awareness of misrepresenting the truth or stealing from the employer are the result of the Holy Spirit's convicting of sin.

When negative circumstances come into our lives, we must allow them to stimulate an evaluation. If the Holy Spirit convicts of some specific wrong, then correction must be made. If the Holy Spirit does not bring some specific conviction to mind, then we can conclude that those circumstances are simply the result of being involved in the sanctification process.

When pleasing circumstances enter our lives, they can heighten our awareness of God's goodness and our need for gratitude.

The tendency to use circumstances to determine whether God is pleased is a dangerous practice. All Christians are involved in

God's preparation for heaven, and at the heart of that process is the life of faith. Sometimes faith can produce positive circumstances, sometimes negative. The product of an obedient life can be persecution, affliction, and misunderstanding. But when we, by faith, act on what we know to be right, we please God.

THE HOLY SPIRIT

Jesus tells us that the Holy Spirit convicts of "sin and righteousness and judgment" (John 16:8). Such convicting may not necessarily be the product of a direct scriptural command. The Holy Spirit, for example, may convict me that a habit is wrong for me although not specifically prohibited in the Scriptures. The Bible does not prohibit gambling, for example, but I may be convinced through the Holy Spirit's prompting that it is an activity in which I should not engage.

The Holy Spirit not only convicts of sin but also provokes to righteousness. While visiting a Third World country, a person sees the deep poverty of people and the utter hopelessness of their condition. In response that person gives money to a beggar. The Bible does not say that we have to give to everybody that asks, but in that circumstance the person feels that is what God's Spirit would have one do.

Emotion and the Holy Spirit are often easily confused because the Holy Spirit often calls on us to do things that, although not prohibited in the Scriptures, are not expressly commanded. Part of the life of faith is responding to what the Holy Spirit seems to be asking of us. There is no guaranteed method of distinguishing between emotion and the Holy Spirit, no way to eliminate risk. The risk may be minimized, however, by extended time in God's Word. As we feed on the Scriptures, we are prepared to respond properly to the Holy Spirit's leadership.

THE BIBLE

All Scripture is applicable, but not all Scripture is obligatory. The Bible is the primary and most important source of application for the Christian, the standard by which all other sources are evaluated. The Holy Spirit never leads contrary to the Scriptures. All counsel and exhortation, as well as all circumstances, must be evaluated in light of God's Word. The Bible is the final authority in the Christian's life.

If the Bible is a reliable indication of God's purposes, then it becomes our authority. If we say that the Bible is not authoritative, we also say we cannot know what God is like, we do not know what He expects from us, and we do not know how to become all He wants us to be. In short, we embrace not only relativism but also a subjective and fuzzy concept of God.

The Bible provides a source of application in two broad areas: *examples* and *commands*. Examples are not normative; commands are. I can draw my own application from examples, but I am obligated to keep the commands.

EXAMPLES

The Bible affords three kinds of examples: positive, negative, and questionable.

1. *Positive* examples are either supported by a command or in principle follow the spirit of the Scriptures. Those examples that are followed by a command become normative simply because of the command. We note in our Lord Jesus' ministry that He was a man of love. We know that we must follow His example because He says, "A new command I give you: Love one another. As I have loved you, so you must love one another" (John 13:34).

Luke records in the Acts of the Apostles: "All the believers were one in heart and mind. No one claimed that any of his possessions was his own, but they shared everything they had" (Acts 4:32).

This positive example is an expression of generosity. The Bible teaches that we are to be generous but gives no command to share all our possessions in common. We are not obliged to follow this example unless we choose to do so.[1]

2. *Negative* examples include those in the Scriptures that are obviously in contradiction to what the Bible teaches, by precept or in spirit. In Acts 5, for example, Ananias and Sapphira, his wife, kept part of their possessions rather than sharing them with the church. They were sentenced to death, not because they refused to share, but because they lied about it. Such deception is obviously wrong and functions as a source of application for the Christian. A negative example is not obligatory unless supported by a command.

In his first letter to the Corinthians Paul relates a series of negative events surrounding the exodus of Israel from Egypt. He comments, "Now these occurred as examples to keep us from setting our hearts on evil things as they did" (1 Corinthians 10:6).

3. *Questionable* examples are those that we find in the Bible and are left wondering whether we should emulate them or not. Should Sarah have laughed (Genesis 18:9–15) when the Lord brought her news of Isaac's birth? Some believe this to be a laugh of unbelief, others an expression of delight and pleasure.

Was Moses justified in killing the Egyptian (Exodus 2:11) in defense of his fellow Hebrew? The Bible neither rebukes Moses for doing it nor justifies the act. The believer is left to decide.

Examples are a rich source of potential application for the believer. God often uses examples in the Bible to prompt us into thinking about different aspects of our lives. In all cases, however, whether they be positive, negative, or questionable examples, *they must be confirmed by a command to be normative for others.*

---

[1] See Appendix

COMMANDS

Two kinds of commands are revealed in the Scriptures: *individual* and *universal*. Generally speaking, the commands that God gives to individuals are not binding today. In Matthew 17:27, for example, Jesus instructs Peter: "Go to the lake and throw out your line. Take the first fish you catch; open its mouth and you will find a four-drachma coin. Take it and give it to them for my tax and yours." Such commands given by God to individuals in the Bible are to be obeyed by those individuals but are not applicable to others.

Universal commands, however, may be given by God to an individual, but the context clearly indicates that the application is to be made by all of God's people. The last words of our Lord fit into this category: "All authority in heaven and on earth has been given to me. Therefore go and make disciples of all nations, baptizing them in the name of the Father and of the Son and of the Holy Spirit, and teaching them to obey everything I have commanded you. And surely I am with you always, to the very end of the age" (Matthew 28:18–20).

Although Jesus gave these words to the disciples, they are applicable to all believers in every age. The command fits into the whole mosaic of Christ's teaching and strategy, and since it was given before the founding of the church at Pentecost, the command is for individuals rather than the corporate body.

Sorting out the various sources of application in the Scriptures becomes more difficult when we address the question, "Which of the universal commands are applicable for our day and age and which were applicable for an earlier day but not for us?" Were the commands given to the nation of Israel applicable for Christians today; if so, which ones; if not, which ones?

Are Christians commanded to sacrifice today? Unanimously the answer would be no. The sacrificial system was done away with after the sacrifice of Jesus. What about feast days? Are we to keep such holy days as the Feast of Tabernacles? Paul seems to indicate that those are likewise cancelled by the finished work of Christ (Colossians 2:14–17).

Are we to abstain from eating pork and shellfish as the dietary laws command? The Scriptures are not quite as explicit on this issue, but many believe that the vision of the great sheet let down from heaven and shown to Peter in Acts 10:9–16 indicates that the things called unclean in the Old Testament are now considered clean.

When we ask, "How shall we handle the observance of the Sabbath Day?" we move into an area of controversy. Many in the church today would argue that Sunday is the New Testament "Sabbath"—or at least the "Lord's Day"—even though Paul says that we are not obliged to keep the Sabbath (Colossians 2:16). No command in the New Testament requires us to observe one day out of seven or to make Sunday the day of worship. As a matter of fact, the commandment to keep the Sabbath given to Moses during the exodus was not a commandment to worship but a commandment to rest. Scripture does not indicate that Israel used the Sabbath as a day of worship, whereas our emphasis on the importance of "observing the Sabbath" or "Lord's Day," is an emphasis on worship rather than rest.

The Mosaic Law is divided into three parts: ceremonial, civil, and moral. Although this is an accurate and convenient delineation between the parts of the Mosaic Law, nowhere in the Old or New Testament is such a delineation used. When Paul states in his epistles that we are no longer under the law, he is, in fact, referring to the whole law of Moses, not just part of it.

CHARTING THE COMMANDS OF SCRIPTURE

As we wrestle with the question of what portions of the commands are obligatory for us today, we can divide the Bible into four sections: (1) the period between Adam and Moses, (2) the period between Moses and Christ, (3) the time of Christ, and (4) the period between the death of Christ until His return.

	Salvation	Obligation	Instruction
Adam to Moses	No Law—Grace	Natural Law?	
Moses to Christ	No Law—Grace	Mosaic Law	
Days of Christ	No Law—Grace	Teachings of Jesus, Mosaic Law	
After Christ	No Law—Grace	Teachings of Jesus N.T. Commands	Mosaic Law

1. *Before Moses:* We do not know the exact duration of this period, but it spans the time from the Garden of Eden to Moses' assignment from God to redeem the children of Israel. In the chart under "Salvation," we find "No Law—Grace." The Bible teaches that salvation is always by grace through faith in Christ. In the Old Testament, people were saved by faith in Christ who was *to come;* in the New Testament people were saved by faith in Christ who has *already come.* Jesus said: "I am the way and the truth and the life. No one comes to the Father except through me" (John 14:6).

Under "Obligation" we find "Natural Law?" The word "law" appears only twice before the time of Moses. In Genesis 47:26, we find: "So Joseph established it as a law concerning land in Egypt." The word for law here is *khoke* and means an "enactment, custom, decree, set time, or statute." It is not the word used to denote those statutes and commandments given by God to Moses. That word in Hebrew is *torah.*

The other use of the word "law" before Moses' time is in Genesis 26:5 and uses the word "torah." It appears in a commentary on Abraham's life rather than a command given by God to His people. God speaks: "I will make your descendants as numerous as the stars in the sky and will give them all these lands, and through your offspring all nations on earth will be blessed, because Abraham obeyed me and kept my requirements, my commands, my decrees, and my laws" (Genesis 26:4–5).

Although the word "law" before Moses is not used in reference to God's giving commands to His people, certain universal commands are given in this period. Before the fall of Adam and Eve, "God blessed them and said to them, 'Be fruitful and increase in number; fill the earth and subdue it. Rule over the fish of the sea and the birds of the air and over every living creature that moves on the ground" (Genesis 1:28).

God gives a group of universal commands to Noah and his descendants in Genesis 9:1–7. Although not called "law," four basic commands are given:

1. A reiteration of the command given in Genesis 1:28.
2. Permission to eat all creatures.
3. Prohibition against eating blood.
4. Prohibition against man's killing man.

Although these were the only universal commands given before the time of Moses, there must have been what we call "natural law." There are incidents that lead us to believe people knew right from wrong, such as the flood and the destruction of Sodom and Gomorrah. Paul refers to this "natural law," which are certain absolutes written on the consciences of people. "When Gentiles, who do not have the law, do by nature things required by the law, they are a law for themselves, even though they do not have the law, since they show that the requirements of the law are written on their hearts, their consciences also bearing witness, and their thoughts now accusing, now even defending them" (Romans 2:14–15).

Sacrifice is introduced after the fall of man (Genesis 4). God does not reveal what He said to Adam and Eve as He inaugurated it. As we see it in operation, however, we can deduce that first, it was an expression of God's grace rather than part of the law. Man sinned, and God instituted the sacrificial system. The hope of God's people was expressed in sacrifice. Second, because sacrifice was an acknowledgment of sin, there must have been an acknowledgment of wrong-doing even though the word "law" (torah) as used by Moses is absent and the universal commands are few. Example rather than command is the source of application during this period.

2. *Moses to Christ:* People during the period from Moses to Christ were also saved by grace. All people in all times have been saved by grace through faith in Christ apart from works.

All the people God calls "great" in the Scriptures—both Old and New Testaments—related to Him on the basis of grace. Even Moses, the great "law giver," refused to relate to God on the basis of the law. So also, David, Daniel, and many others insisted on relating to God on the basis of grace. They understood God's grace. Therefore, David could say, "I delight in your decrees; I will not neglect your word" (Psalm 119:16). He could delight in God's law because his relationship with God was based on grace, not his own performance.

Under "Obligation" is listed the "Mosaic Law," the law given by God to Israel through Moses. Most of it, including the Ten Commandments, was enacted on Mount Sinai in the forty-day period that Moses was with God.

Not all the law, however, was given to Moses at that time. The word *torah,* for example, appears for the first time in the Old Testament as a law given by God to man in Exodus 12:49. Israel is still in bondage in Egypt, and God is instituting the Passover. The Lord says to Moses, "The same law applies to the native-born and to the alien living among you."

Hebrews 10:1–4 gives us two reasons for the Mosaic Law: "The law is only a shadow of the good things that are coming—

not the realities themselves. For this reason it can never, by the same sacrifices repeated endlessly year after year, make perfect those who draw near to worship. If it could, would they not have stopped being offered? For the worshipers would have been cleansed once for all, and would no longer have felt guilty for their sins. But those sacrifices are an annual reminder of sins, because it is impossible for the blood of bulls and goats to take away sins."

The law was given: (1) to show the inadequacy of man's way, and (2) to present a picture of God's way. The frequency of the sacrifices by the same person at the same place was a vivid reminder that the blood of animals could not atone for sin; the author uses the words "shadow" and "image" to show that the sacrificial system was a preview of the perfect sacrifice of Jesus Christ.

3. *Days of Christ:* The Gospels represent the transition from the Old Covenant to the New. Jesus did not seek to minister to the Gentiles, and He was very pointed in saying so (Matthew 10:5-7). His ministry was exclusively to the Jews. Yet Jesus did not call the Jews to the law but to Himself. Still Christ was very careful to keep the Mosaic Law and told His audience that they must keep it as well.

In the Sermon on the Mount, He said: "Do not think that I have come to abolish the Law or the Prophets; I have not come to abolish them but to fulfill them. I tell you the truth, until heaven and earth disappear, not the smallest letter, not the least stroke of a pen, will by any means disappear from the Law until everything is accomplished. Anyone who breaks one of the least of these commandments and teaches others to do the same will be called least in the kingdom of heaven, but whoever practices and teaches these commands will be called great in the kingdom of heaven" (Matthew 5:17-19).

Here Jesus stated that He did not come to destroy the law but to fulfill it. He fulfilled it in the sense that He *was* the fulfillment of what the law had promised, and He fulfilled it in the sense that only He kept the law perfectly.

The New Testament word for law is *nomos* from which we get our English words "nomian" (law) and "antinomian" (against the law). The law here obviously refers to Mosaic Law, since there was no law before the days of Moses. In the Sermon on the Mount, however, Jesus adds a new dimension to the Mosaic Law. A proper attitude, humility, dependence, submission, and purity of motive are stressed along with the outward keeping of the law.

We must remember that in Matthew 5:19 Jesus is speaking to Jews who are obliged to keep the law; otherwise, we will misunderstand what Scripture teaches. Paul taught that Moses' commandments were ineffective since we are no longer under the Mosaic Law (Colossians 2:14–17). *If verse 19 of Matthew 5 is applicable in the "post-Christ" period, we have to conclude that Paul is "least in the kingdom of Heaven,"* for he taught people to break the law.

Even as Jesus emphasizes the importance of keeping the Mosaic Law (having kept it fully Himself), He sets the tone of His sermon and of His whole ministry in Matthew 5:1–12, commonly called "The Beatitudes." Although Jesus kept the Mosaic Law and taught His Jewish audience that they, too, were obliged to keep it, He did not *call* people to keep the law per se but to follow Him. As the fulfillment of the law, Jesus was the one who should be followed.

Therefore, during the days of Christ, (1) Jesus fulfilled the Mosaic Law; (2) He taught the Jews to whom He ministered that they, like He, must keep the law; (3) as the fulfillment of the law, He, not the law, was to be their hope; (4) He called people to follow Him, not the law. We can conclude that (1) we are to follow Jesus as well and consider His teachings and commands as obligatory; (2) we are *not* obliged to keep the law which He kept and which He taught the Jews of His day to keep, because we are not under the law but under grace.

In the Old Testament, God had an institutional as well as an individual commitment to Israel. Not all Jews were believers and therefore saved, but irrespective of how few the believing Jews of Israel might be, God's commitment to the institution of Israel was irrevocable.

In the New Testament, God has no institutional commitment, only individual commitment. He is not committed to the institution of the Roman Catholic Church, the Presbyterians, the Baptists, or the Methodists. As He was to the nation of Israel, He is only committed to those who have put their trust in Christ. In the Old Testament, the law, which had to be obeyed by individuals was given to the nation of Israel. In the New Testament, there is no institutional commitment on the part of God and, therefore, no need for the Old Testament law.

Because Jesus provides the transition between the Old and New Testaments, for the purpose of application a distinction must be maintained between the teachings and commands of Jesus on the one hand and His emphasis on the law on the other.

4. *After Christ:* The word "law" finds a place in the New Testament, but it is used quite differently than in the Old Testament. Three times (Romans 13:8–10, Galatians 5:14, and James 2:8) the believer is urged to keep the "law of love," not the Mosaic Law. We are told that all the Mosaic Law is fulfilled by the keeping of this "law of love." The emphasis of our Savior is that the heart of the law is an attitude of love.

We are told to keep the "law" in Acts and in the epistles, but it is never the Mosaic law. Rather it is the "law that gives freedom" (James 1:25), the "law of Christ" (Galatians 6:2), the "law of the spirit of life through Christ Jesus" (Romans 8:2).

We are told that we are not under the law but under grace (Romans 6:14)—that is, we are free from the Mosaic Law. In this passage Paul does not suggest that we are free to sin but free to become servants of Christ. The freedom of the believer after the Cross is the freedom of the believer before Sinai. It is a relationship with God apart from law. People in this period who are living in the liberty of Christ are no more antinomian than Abraham was.

We relate to the Mosaic law in that we are to "be instructed by it." In 1 Corinthians 10:1–15 Paul refers to the Mosaic period. In verse 6 he says, "Now these things occurred as examples, to keep us from setting our hearts on evil things as they did." Again in verse 11 he repeats the same idea: "These things happened to them as examples and were written down as warnings for us, on whom the fulfillment of the ages has come."

The Mosaic Law is an important source of application for Christians. We are to learn from it and be instructed by it, but we are not obliged to keep it. We are obliged to keep Jesus' teachings with the exception of the law of Moses and we are obliged to keep the New Testament commands.

SUMMARY

The six sources of application are obedience to an authority, counsel, the thoughts and challenges of people, circumstances, the Holy Spirit, and the Bible. The Bible is the primary and most important source for the believer, and we use it in application in the following ways:

In the period from Adam to Moses, we learn primarily from the examples, since there are no laws stated except the few universal commands.

In the 1,500-year period from Moses to Christ, Israel lived under the Mosaic Law. As Christians under the New Covenant, we are not under the law and, therefore, not obliged to keep it. It is available for our edification and instruction, and we can learn from it. It is a rich source of application for the Christian, but the commands, like the examples, are an individual matter as far as obedience is concerned.

The period of the Gospels surrounding Christ's life represents a period of transition from the Old Covenant to the New. The people in the days of the Lord Jesus were obliged to keep both the teachings of Jesus and the Mosaic Law. The Gospels are a rich source of application in that we are to follow the teachings of Jesus, but we are not obliged to follow the Mosaic Law. Jesus kept the Mosaic Law for the purpose of fulfilling the law. In short, Jesus did what we are neither obliged nor able to do. From the death of Christ until His return, we are to follow the New Testament commands. The examples in this period, as in the other three periods, are instructional but not obligatory.

Application is rooted in the conviction that, although a passage has but one meaning, it has many applications. Application is preceded by a proper interpretation, but interpretation is always followed by application. The passage may be interpreted to apply to other ages or situations, such as the Mosaic Law, but the believer can still derive a Spirit-directed application from it today.

The examples of Scripture may be positive, negative, or questionable. They must, however, be reinforced by a Scriptural command to be normative.

Commands, on the other hand, can be either universal or individual. We must study the Bible so that we can understand the difference between individual and universal commands. All Scripture is applicable, but not all Scripture is obligatory.

PRINCIPLES FOR MEDITATION

18. Culture cannot serve as an excuse for not obeying God's commands.

25. We must maintain an accountability relationship with a group of people who will exhort us to faith and good works.

26. Godly counsel is helpful in the quest for obedience, but it should never be used to avoid personal responsibility.

QUESTIONS FOR DISCUSSION

1. What portions of the Bible are obligatory for all people today?

2. How would you answer a person who said, "We are obligated to follow the example of Jesus Christ." Amplify why you would give the answer you do.

3. Explain in your own words the correlation between the source of application and the *process* of application.

SECTION III

The Principles of Application

10 Foundation Principles of Application

CERTAIN FOUNDATIONAL TRUTHS MUST BE EMBRACED TO BEGIN THE PROCESS OF OBEDIENCE.

In all endeavors, foundational truths must be understood before the effort is begun. In business, the customer is always right. This credo has been the guideline for many corporations over the last hundred years, and it is foundational to all efforts and decisions made within such companies.

Scriptural application is based on foundational truths as well. The following rules are foundational principles for any consideration of Scriptural application:

1. Application must be focused on pleasing God rather than pleasing others.

2. Every problem a person has is related to his or her concept of God.

3. Attitude is as important as action in obeying God's commands.

4. Surrender is the cornerstone of all application. Refusal to surrender blurs our ability to discover and do God's will.

5. Application is a process, not a single event.

An understanding of these principles is essential in beginning the process of obedience.

RULE ONE

Application must be focused on pleasing God rather than pleasing others.

The author of Hebrews reminds us that the descendants of Aaron were well suited to be priests. The priest's ability to identify with people is one of the subjects of Hebrews 5: "He is able to deal gently with those who are ignorant and are going astray, since he himself is subject to weakness" (Hebrews 5:2).

Empathy with the people was possible for these Old Testament priests simply because they were plagued with the same problem—sin. For that reason, they couldn't help the people. A sinner cannot impart righteousness to another sinner.

The solution to man's sin problem had to be found in "one who has been tempted in every way, just as we are—yet was without sin" (Hebrews 4:15). That is, He had to be a man who could understand our problem, but not have the problem.

In our quest for godliness we must seek to emulate the "Perfect High Priest" rather than a priest "from among men." This is for two reasons. First, people inevitably establish extrabiblical standards for us and judge our spirituality on the basis of our conformity to their standards. Second, when we do meet their expectations, they will cease nudging us towards Christlikeness.

The Scribes and Pharisees of Jesus' day established rules and regulations not found in the Bible. These became normative not only for the religious leaders but also for all who would be godly. Jesus felt no obligation to keep these extra-biblical standards. He did obey the laws of the Scriptures, as He Himself testified: "Do not think that I have come to abolish the Law or the Prophets; I have not come to abolish them but to fulfill them" (Matthew 5:17).

But keeping the Old Testament statutes was not enough for these custodians of right and wrong. They expected Jesus to follow their rules as well. The Savior's refusal was a major reason the Sanhedrin wanted Him dead. If the focus of Jesus' application had been toward pleasing men rather than God, He would have become a Pharisee.

Mores and taboos change from generation to generation. In the nineteenth century, for instance, most of the evangelical churches in the United States taught that drinking tea and coffee was wrong. Often these man-made rules not only add to, but clash with God's laws. On this subject, Jesus said to the Pharisees: "You have a fine way of setting aside the commands of God in order to observe your own traditions! For Moses said, 'Honor your father and mother,' and, 'Anyone who curses his father or mother must be put to death.' But you say that if a man says to his father or mother: 'Whatever help you might otherwise have received from me is Corban' (that is, a gift devoted to God), then you no longer let him do anything for his father or mother. Thus you nullify the word of God by your tradition that you have handed down. And you do many things like that" (Mark 7:9–13).

When we meet the expectations of people, they cease to nudge us toward Christlikeness. Converted out of a life of debauchery, Jean becomes part of the believing fellowship. Her past lifestyle is unacceptable to any moral individual—much less to the church. So, pressure is exerted on Jean to "clean up her act." Within a couple of years she fits very nicely into her new-found environment. Her lifestyle matches that of the congregation.

Now the pressure is off. Jean is a member in good standing, and her fellow Christians' expectations are met. No longer do they exhort her to godliness; she is as godly as they are.

Does this mean that the Holy Spirit is satisfied and that the sanctification process has come to an end? Not at all. As long as Jean compares herself with her fellow believers, her spiritual ears will be dulled; for instance, she may lie and be reluctant to confess it. If her application focus is on meeting God's expectations, she will jump the hurdle of her reluctance, obey the Holy Spirit's nudging, and rectify her wrong. But if the focus of her application is people, she will justify her wrong, suppress the convicting voice of the Holy Spirit, and walk away from application.

The focus of our application must be toward pleasing God rather than pleasing others.

RULE TWO

Every problem a person has is related to his or her concept of God.

Not only is God sovereign and in control, He also has believers' best interests at heart as He monitors the flow of circumstances through their lives. As Joseph's life unfolds in the book of Genesis, we see God manipulating history to accomplish His own goals.

In Genesis 37:28 Joseph's brothers sell him to a Midianite caravan on its way to Egypt. In 39:1, the captain of Pharaoh's guard buys Joseph. By verse 20 Joseph is in prison because of the wiles of Potiphar's wife. Genesis 40 records that Pharaoh's butler and baker are cast into the same prison. Because Joseph has maintained a good attitude, he is trusted, and the butler and baker come under Joseph's care. When the butler and the baker have mysterious dreams, Joseph interprets them, predicting the restoration of the butler and the demise of the baker. The butler is restored.

Now Pharaoh has a dream (Genesis 41). No one can interpret it, and the butler suggests that Joseph might be able to help. Joseph interprets the dream for Pharaoh and ends up becoming Egypt's prime minister. In the morning Joseph is in prison; that afternoon he is in the palace—a clear illustration of God ordering events to accomplish His own purpose.

At the end of Joseph's life his testimony to his brothers is: "You intended to harm me, but God intended it for good to accomplish what is now being done, the saving of many lives" (Genesis 50:20).

Joseph's story is an illustration of the biblical teaching that God is in control and has our best interests at heart. Other people cannot hurt us except by divine permission. This principle does not absolve others of their responsibility, but it does mean that when I have a problem, my problem is with God, not with others.

David's response in the Psalms also illustrates this truth. In Psalm 18:16–19, he testifies:

> He reached down from on high and took hold of me;
>   he drew me out of deep waters.
> He rescued me from my powerful enemy,
>   from my foes, who were too strong for me.
> They confronted me in the day of my disaster,
>   but the LORD was my support.
> He brought me out into a spacious place;
>   he rescued me because he delighted in me.

When things are going poorly for David and when his enemies seem to be gaining on him, he takes his case before God. He does not, however, simply abandon the issue; a recognition of God's control is never an excuse for inactivity.

Frequently the Bible calls on us to respond to circumstances differently than we would naturally want to respond. When we bless our enemies or turn the other cheek or go to war, the application of the Scriptures requires risk taking—first because we do not know how the situation will turn out; second, because application runs counter to how we naturally feel. As Job goes through the trauma of defending himself from his friends as they challenge his integrity, he cries out for an opportunity to take his case directly to God. Time and again he expresses a longing to confront God with some difficult questions. When he finally meets God and is given the opportunity to address the issue, he declines. He merely says, "My ears had heard of you but now my eyes have seen you. Therefore I despise myself and repent in dust and ashes" (Job 42:5–6). When Job met God, his problems appeared superfluous.

Every problem in life requires an application of the Scriptures, either in attitude or in conduct. How we respond will be determined by our concept of God.

RULE THREE

Attitude is as important as action in obeying God's commands.

Twice during Saul's brief reign in Israel the prophet Samuel came with a reprimand from God. The first, in 1 Samuel 13, occurs before the battle with the Philistines. Israel's army, arrayed for battle, waited for Samuel to come and offer a sacrifice on their behalf.

He waited seven days, the time set by Samuel; but Samuel did not come to Gilgal, and Saul's men began to scatter. So he said, "Bring me the burnt offering and the fellowship offerings." And Saul offered up the burnt offering. Just as he finished making the offering, Samuel arrived, and Saul went out to greet him.

"What have you done?" asked Samuel.

Saul replied, "When I saw that the men were scattering, and that you did not come at the set time, and that the Philistines were assembling at Micmash, I thought, 'Now the Philistines will come down against me at Gilgal, and I have not sought the LORD's favor. So I felt compelled to offer the burnt offering." "You acted foolishly," Samuel said. "You have not kept the command the LORD your God gave you; if you had, he would have established your kingdom over Israel for all time. But now your kingdom will not endure; the LORD has sought out a man after his own heart and appointed him leader of his people, because you have not kept the LORD's command." (1 Samuel 13:8–14)

This was not the first time a non-Levite intruded into the priest's office, nor would it be the last. Gideon, Jephthah, and Elijah all offered sacrifices with impunity, and Scripture gives no indication that they were related to Levi.

Samuel's second rebuke followed Saul's return from fighting the Amalekites. God had sent Saul to avenge the way Amalek had treated Israel during the exodus. God commanded Saul to destroy the Amalekites. "When Samuel reached him, Saul said, 'The LORD bless you; I have carried out the LORD's instructions'" (1 Samuel 15:13). Saul claims to have kept God's commandment, and in a sense he did. He merely saved some of the spoil for a future sacrifice.

In both encounters, no moral issue was at stake, as there was in the case of King David when he committed adultery with Bathsheba and murdered her husband, Uriah (2 Samuel 11). Saul had not broken one of the Ten Commandments. Yet Saul was alienated from God the rest of his life while God calls David "a man after my own heart" (Acts 13:22).

The issue is deeper than the actions of these two men; the difference relates to their attitudes toward God.

Samuel reproves Saul for his disobedience: "Does the LORD delight in burnt offerings and sacrifices as much as in obeying the voice of the LORD? To obey is better than sacrifice, and to heed is better than the fat of rams. For rebellion is like the sin of divination, and arrogance like the evil of idolatry. Because you have rejected the word of the LORD, he has rejected you as king" (1 Samuel 15:22–23).

Rebellion lies at the heart of Samuel's charge. Rebellion and sinful acts are not synonymous; a person can be rebellious and not *do* anything wrong. Conversely, a person can do wrong and not be in rebellion. Rebellion is primarily, though not exclusively, an act of the heart.

In 1 Samuel 15:13 Saul protests to Samuel that obedience was his intent. But he wanted to take God's command and filter it through his own conviction of what was reasonable. Instead of abandoning himself and carrying out God's request, he evaluated it in light of his own value system—and that is rebellion.

Many centuries later, as Jesus and His disciples walked through the grain fields, the Pharisees challenged them for gleaning and eating grain on the Sabbath: "Jesus answered them, 'Have you never read what David did when he and his companions were hungry? He entered the house of God, and taking the consecrated bread, he ate what is lawful only for priests to eat. And he also gave some to his companions.' Then Jesus said to them, 'The Son of Man is Lord of the Sabbath' " (Luke 6:3–5).

To justify the disciples' actions, Jesus referred to the time when David, fleeing from Saul, ate the bread in the tabernacle (see Leviticus 24:5–9 and 1 Samuel 21:1–6). David broke the law, and not only was he not reprimanded for it, but Jesus also excuses it.

Does this mean we can break God's law as long as we have a good attitude? Not at all!

Isaiah addresses this issue in the opening paragraphs of his prophecy:

> "The multitude of your sacrifices—
>   what are they to me?" says the LORD.
> I have more than enough of burnt offerings,
>   of rams and the fat of fattened animals;
> I have no pleasure

in the blood of bulls and lambs and goats.
When you come to meet with me,
     who has asked this of you,
     this trampling of my courts?
Stop bringing meaningless offerings!
     Your incense is detestable to me.
New Moons, Sabbaths and convocations—
     I cannot bear your evil assemblies.
Your New Moon festivals and your appointed feasts
     my soul hates.
They have become a burden to me;
     I am weary of bearing them.
When you spread out your hands in prayer,
     I will hide my eyes from you;
even if you offer many prayers,
     I will not listen.
Your hands are full of blood;
     wash and make yourselves clean.
Take your evil deeds
     out of my sight!
Stop doing wrong,
     learn to do right!
Seek justice,
     encourage the oppressed.
Defend the cause of the fatherless,
     plead the case of the widow.

"Come now, let us reason together,"
     says the LORD.
"Though your sins are like scarlet,
     they shall be as white as snow;
though they are red as crimson,
     they shall be like wool.
If you are willing and obedient,
     you will eat the best from the land;
but if you resist and rebel,
     you will be devoured by the sword."

For the mouth of the Lord has spoken.

(Isaiah 1:11–20)

Israel, in a perfunctory fashion, kept the ceremonial and sacrificial aspects of the law. The people's hearts, however, were not in their obedience, because they failed to keep the law's "weightier matters." Isaiah told them to abandon their ritualistic practices, but he did not suggest that they stop keeping the moral law.

God summarizes his complaint against Israel in Isaiah: "These people come near to me with their mouth and honor me with their lips, but their hearts are far from me. Their worship of me is made up only of rules taught by men" (Isaiah 29:13). Nowhere does the prophet imply that, since God does not have His people's hearts, they can stop keeping His commandments.

Proper action is important to God, but that action should be based on a spirit of dependence and submission. As long as I vote on a command's reasonableness and modify it based on how I evaluate it, I am in rebellion. My heart's attitude is as important as my action in obeying God's commands.

RULE FOUR

Surrender is the cornerstone of all application. Refusal to surrender blurs our ability to discover and do God's will.

We can easily see the connection between surrender to God and applying His commandments. We obey what He says because we are submissive to Him, and we are in submission to Him because of who He is.

Many of the New Testament epistles are written from this perspective; Ephesians is a case in point. The first three chapters remind us who Jesus Christ is and what He did for us. Beginning with chapter four, we are told of our responsibility. Because He is Lord, we are to submit to His expectations. The last three chapters enumerate the various applications expected.

Although the connection between surrender to God and knowing His will is not readily apparent, it is nonetheless compelling. To help the believer discover and do God's will, God provides counsel through proven people and leads through the Scriptures and the Holy Spirit. These indicators become blurred, however, if the believer does not seek God's will with a submissive attitude.

Hebrews 3 discusses Israel's sojourn to Canaan after years of slavery in Egypt. Quoting from Psalm 95, the author says: "Do not harden your hearts as you did in the rebellion, during the time of testing in the desert, where your fathers tested and tried me and for forty years saw what I did" (Hebrews 3:8–9).

In verse 8, God tested them; in verse 9, Israel tested God. The controversy was the giants in Canaan—God wanted Israel to face the giants, but Israel did not want to. Both God and Israel had Israel's best uppermost in their minds. Conflict resulted from disagreeing on what that best interest looked like. The Bible is filled with assurances that God loves His children and designs all circumstances so that they contribute to the children's good. Paul assures the Romans: "And we know that in all things God works for the good of those who love him, who have been called according to his purpose" (Romans 8:28).

We question God's commitment to us either when events we don't like invade our lives or when we suspect God is asking us to do something we don't want to do. Circumstances we don't like frequently interrupt our lives with varying degrees of magnitude. On a recent trip to Fort Campbell, a soldier sought counsel from me on how to handle a tragedy. He had just returned from overseas, and his wife and two daughters were driving to meet him. A drunk lost control of his vehicle, crossed the lane, hit the car, and the young soldier's family burned to death in the accident. "If God truly loves us and is in control, why did He allow this to happen?" the distraught soldier asked.

God is not obliged to tell His children why such things happen. He rarely takes us into His confidence with what we consider is an adequate explanation. He does assure us, however, that He is in control, that there is purpose behind such events, that He loves us and has our best interests at heart. Believing this without understanding why is faith. Our confidence is in God's character rather than our ability to understand why He does what He does. If our submission to Him is based on our ability to understand His ways, we will wander in the wilderness of confusion just as Israel did when they refused to fight the giants.

All of us have chuckled at the *Peanuts* sequence in which Lucy holds the football for Charlie Brown, only to pull it away at the last minute. Wary of a repeat performance, he extracts from her assurances that she won't pull the ball away next time. Having been placated with soothing words, he tries again. Each time she jerks the ball away, and each time Charlie Brown slams to the ground.

When circumstances go awry, the tendency is to question God's commitment. We feel we have entered into a Charlie Brown–Lucy relationship with God in which we are never sure if God is going to pull away the football as we try to kick it. The next step, withholding our submission to God, is a short one.

Surrender is the cornerstone of all application, and it is based on our concept of God. If He is sovereign and has our best interests at heart, then we can submit to Him assured that, although we may not know why He does what He does, his loving purpose rules. The only tragedy in life we need fear is the tragedy of self-will.

In addition to questioning God's commitment to us when circumstances are difficult, we also may question His goodness when we fear He may ask us to do something we don't want to do. A graduating high-school student was accepted at several different colleges. He prayed about the one he should accept and sought counsel from people who knew and loved him. Weeks turned into months, and still he didn't know where to go. What was God's will?

The roadblock was his lack of neutrality. He couldn't look his Lord in the face and say, "Thy will be done," because he didn't want to attend one of the colleges and feared that, if he surrendered, God would ask him to go there. Normally a confident, decisive person, he found himself in the valley of indecision, desperately trying to climb out—on his own terms. His refusal to surrender blurred his ability to discover and do God's will.

RULE FIVE <hr> **Application is a process, not a single event.**	This principle is the heart of understanding biblical application. We have seen it illustrated in the lives of such people as Rebekah, Rahab, Joseph, Saul, Daniel, and Jesus; it is further illustrated by Abraham.

Abraham is one of the recognized "greats" in the Bible; he is referred to no less than seventy-five times in the New Testament. In Genesis, however, we find that he led a rather uneventful life. He wrote no books; he built no cities; he made no great discoveries; he did not become a ruler. He simply lived.

In the morning Abraham got up, sat in front of his tent, probably gave some instruction to his herdsmen, and went to bed at night. Periodically he moved from Shechem to Peniel, from Peniel to Hebron, from Hebron back to Shechem. He did have an adventurous moment when he saved Lot from his enemies (Genesis 14). But most of the time he simply believed God's promises and waited for God to fulfill them.

Abraham is not great in the economy of God because of what he did; he didn't do much! He is great because: "Abram believed the LORD, and he credited it to him as righteousness" (Genesis 15:6).

Many of God's greats were significant leaders. In God's Hall of Fame in Hebrews 11, many great leaders are mentioned. Joseph, for example, became prime minister of Egypt, but Hebrews says he was great because: "By faith Joseph, when his end was near, spoke about the exodus of the Israelites from Egypt and gave instructions about his bones" (Hebrews 11:22).

Moses, obviously a great man, led the children of Israel out of captivity and was God's vehicle for communicating the law. But God considered him great because of his faith: "By faith Moses, when he had grown up, refused to be known as the son of Pharaoh's daughter. He chose to be mistreated along with the people of God rather than to enjoy the pleasures of sin for a short time. He regarded disgrace for the sake of Christ as of greater value than the treasures of Egypt, because he was looking ahead to his reward. By faith he left Egypt, not fearing the king's anger; he persevered because he saw him who is invisible. By faith he kept the Passover and the sprinkling of blood, so that the destroyer of the firstborn would not touch the firstborn of Israel" (Hebrews 11:24–28).

Nowhere in Hebrews 11 are people considered great because of worldly accomplishments. All these men and women were great because they understood God's program and were willing participants. In short, they were process-oriented rather than product-oriented.

Abraham and those who followed him as God's "greats" did not view application as a single event. They did not try to evaluate their holiness on the basis of faithful acts. They understood that walking with God was a day-by-day, moment-by-moment process, and that process included responding properly to what God asked them to do.

For Abraham that process began when God called him: "The LORD had said to Abram, 'Leave your country, your people and

your father's household and go to the land I will show you'"
(Genesis 12:1).

As an act of faith, Abraham cooperated with God in the
process: "By faith Abraham, when called to go to a place he
would later receive as his inheritance, obeyed and went, even
though he did not know where he was going" (Hebrews 11:8).

On entering the promised land, Abraham had not "arrived" in
his relationship with God. When famine hit Canaan, he and
Sarah went to Egypt. Abraham suggested to Sarah: "Say you are
my sister, so that I will be treated well for your sake and my life
will be spared because of you" (Genesis 12:13).

The famine ended, and Abraham returned to Canaan. They
still had not arrived in the process of trusting God. In Gerar, he
takes the same action with Sarah: "And there Abraham said of
his wife Sarah, 'She is my sister.' Then Abimelech king of Gerar
sent for Sarah and took her" (Genesis 20:2).

If Abraham, the man of faith, had arrived in the process, there
would have been no need for God to test him with Isaac: "Some
time later God tested Abraham. He said to him, 'Abraham!'

" 'Here I am,' he replied.

"Then God said, 'Take your son, your only son, Isaac, whom
you love, and go to the region of Moriah. Sacrifice him there as a
burnt offering on one of the mountains I will tell you about'"
(Genesis 22:1–2).

Each step of faith, each testing, prepared Abraham for his next
step with God. Because application is not a single event, at no
time in Abraham's life had he arrived. The same is true for every
believer. Application must be viewed not as a single event, but
as a lifelong process of responding properly to God.

GROUP

11 Principles on Personal Responsibility

CERTAIN COMMITMENTS TO PERSONAL RESPONSIBILITY ARE REQUIRED TO PROCEED IN THE APPLICATION OF SCRIPTURES.

God holds the believer responsible for certain commitments to proceed in personal application. These commitments, coupled with the foundational truths, begin the application process. As with the foundational truths, these commitments must be accepted, understood, and acted on. If we are to accept responsibility for our actions, we must understand what actions are required.

In training children we often deal with the fundamentals, teaching them their basic responsibilities so that they can begin to create habits for good living. This practice holds true in scriptural growth. God has given us specific responsibilities in the application process. Rules 6–10 profile five areas of personal responsibility to which we must commit ourselves:

6. In those areas of life not directly addressed by the Scriptures, we must develop personal convictions to govern our behavior.

7. When applying the Scriptures, we must make a distinction between the positive and negative commandments.

8. Each person is individually responsible for applying the Scriptures to his or her own life.

9. In all things we must be teachable. We must be willing to admit that we are wrong, change direction and appear inconsistent.

10. The acknowledgment of wrong must be followed by restitution when it is within our power.

RULE SIX

In those areas of life not addressed by the Scriptures, we must develop personal convictions to govern our behavior.

The Scriptures specify few prohibitions. If we were to list them, they would scarcely fill more than a page. This is in contrast to most societies, which have volumes of laws. Believers are free to do whatever the Bible does not prohibit. Christians have considerable freedom.

The Word includes no commandments that prohibit gambling, frequenting night clubs, having more than one spouse, or drinking alcoholic beverages. It does not suggest that we *ought* to do these things, of course, but rather, the Bible does not *demand* that we abstain. If the state has no laws governing such behavior, the believer is free to do them.

But to exercise one's freedom in Christ and indulge in all behavior not expressly prohibited by God can cause irreparable harm, as Paul implied when he said, " 'Everything is permissible'—but not everything is beneficial. 'Everything is permissible'—but not everything is constructive'' (1 Corinthians 10:23). Because there are so few negative commands in the Bible, and most of them are self-evident, nonbelievers can and often do abide by them as successfully as believers. If we don't establish limits in areas other than those mentioned in the Bible, we run the risk of becoming emotionally yoked with the world.

While in Midian, Moses encountered God at the burning bush. God commissioned Moses to free Israel from Egyptian slavery. The Lord said: "The elders of Israel will listen to you. Then you and the elders are to go to the king of Egypt and say to him, 'The LORD, the God of the Hebrews, has met with us. Let us take a three-day journey into the desert to offer sacrifices to the LORD our God' " (Exodus 3:18).

Moses went before Pharaoh and repeated God's command: "This is what the LORD , the God of Israel, says: 'Let my people go, so that they may hold a festival to me in the desert' " (Exodus 5:1).

As the plagues increased in intensity, Pharaoh began to compromise with Moses. Israel can sacrifice to the Lord, he said, but not leave Egypt. "Then the Pharaoh summoned Moses and Aaron and said, 'Go, sacrifice to your God here in the land' " (Exodus 8:25).

During the negotiations, Pharaoh sought accommodation, and Moses *increased* the demand: "Then Pharaoh summoned Moses and said, 'Go, worship the LORD. Even your women and children may go with you; only leave your flocks and herds behind.'

"But Moses said, 'You must allow us to have sacrifices and burnt offerings to present to the LORD our God. Our livestock too must go with us; not a hoof is to be left behind. We have to use some of them in worshiping the LORD our God, and until we get

there we will not know what we are to use to worship the LORD' "
(Exodus 10:24–26).

The Lord did not say that the flocks and herds had to go. This
was Moses' idea—his conviction. He went beyond what God
required, and God backed him.

The same principle can be seen in Daniel's life. Darius had
decreed that for thirty days people could worship only the king.
"Now when Daniel learned that the decree had been published,
he went home to his upstairs room where the windows opened
toward Jerusalem. Three times a day he got down on his knees
and prayed, giving thanks to his God, just as he had done
before" (Daniel 6:10).

Nothing in Scripture requires a person to have devotions three
times a day. Daniel could have said, "I'll get up early and have
my quiet time before the rest of the city rises." Or he could have
shut the windows. Scripture even suggests that the windows be
closed: "When you pray, do not be like the hypocrites, for they
love to pray standing in the synagogues and on the street corners
to be seen by men. I tell you the truth, they have received their
reward in full. But when you pray, go into your room, close the
door and pray to your Father, who is unseen. Then your Father,
who sees what is done in secret, will reward you" (Matthew
6:5–6).

To pray three times a day with the windows open was *Daniel's*
idea. Evidently it pleased God. When Daniel was caught and
sentenced to the lion's den, the Lord closed the lions' mouths.

As we seek to obey the Lord, we are to be sensitive to the
Holy Spirit's leading. Part of that leading relates to prohibitions
not mentioned in the Bible.

We have some good friends who feel they should not join the
country club. They can afford it, but they feel they shouldn't
belong. Others that we know, equally godly, belong to country
clubs.

The Holy Spirit may prohibit one Christian from doing

something while allowing another to do it. I must resist the temptation to judge others as less spiritual because they do what the Lord has forbidden me to do.

At times, evangelical Christians have tended to make biblical absolutes out of such issues as gambling, drinking alcohol, and dancing. Failure to comply brought condemnation, and the system resulted in Pharisaism. We should formulate our own convictions, but we should not make them normative for others.

Our generation is freer; the environment is healthier. But now we err in allowing our freedom to become license. Those who have a heart for application must develop God-given convictions in those areas of life not addressed by the Scriptures.

RULE SEVEN

When applying the Scriptures, we must make a distinction between the positive and negative commandments.

By and large, negative commandments deal with what we are to do away with. Positive commands state what we are to add in our lives. Negative commandments tend to be clear, crisp, and easy to evaluate. In contrast, positive commandments tend to be nebulous and difficult to evaluate.

Paul, in his letter to the Colossians notes the difference between positive commandments and negative commandments:

Put to death, therefore, whatever belongs to your earthly nature: sexual immorality, impurity, lust, evil desires and greed, which is idolatry. Because of these, the wrath of God is coming. You used to walk in these ways, in the life you once lived. But now you must rid yourself of all such things as these: anger, rage, malice, slander, and filthy language from your lips. Do not lie to each other, since you have taken off your old self with its practices and have put on the new self, which is being renewed in knowledge in the image of its Creator. Here there is no Greek or Jew, circumcised or uncircumcised, barbarian, Scythian, slave or free, but Christ is all, and is in all.

Therefore, as God's chosen people, holy and dearly loved, clothe yourselves with compassion, kindness, humility, gentleness and patience. Bear with each other and forgive whatever grievances you may have against one another. Forgive as the Lord forgave you. And over all these virtues put on love, which binds them all together in perfect unity.

Let the peace of Christ rule in your hearts, since as members of one body you were called to peace. And be thankful. Let the word of Christ dwell in you richly as you teach and admonish one another in all wisdom, and as you sing psalms, hymns and spiritual songs with gratitude in your hearts to God. And whatever you do, whether in word or deed, do it all in the name of the Lord Jesus, giving thanks to God the Father through him. (Colossians 3:5–17)

In verse 5, Paul says that we are not to commit fornication. We all know immediately whether or not we have broken this negative commandment. Again, in verse 9, he says: "Do not lie to each other." When evaluating ourselves in light of all the negative commandments, we know immediately where we stand because they tend to deal with conduct.

Not so with the positive commandments. In Colossians 3:12, Paul says we are to be compassionate, kind, humble, patient. If we ask ourselves, "Am I humble?" in all probability we would have a difficult time answering. We would hesitate and say that we try to be but are more humble at some times than at others, and maybe not as humble as we should be or possibly more humble than we used to be. The positive commandments deal with heart attitudes, making evaluation difficult, if not impossible. A person can obey the command "thou shalt not kill" but have a bad attitude in the process.

Sometimes we can use the negative commandments in evaluating the positive commandments. The Bible says, for example, that I am to love my wife—a positive commandment. The Bible also says that I am not to divorce my wife—a negative commandment. If I love my wife, I will not divorce her. The negative commandment serves as a guide in helping me to evaluate the positive one. But this approach has obvious limitations because it is a one-way street. If I love my wife, I will not divorce her. Yet just because I have not divorced my wife does not mean that I love her.

Both positive and negative commandments require personal application. Whenever we apply the Scriptures we look for some way to evaluate how we are doing. The negative commandments make that task easy through objective evaluation. With the positive commandments, objective evaluation is impossible; all evaluation of the positive commandments is subjective. We must be careful in evaluating our success in keeping the positive commandments. If we seek to apply objective standards of measurement to them, we will either become guilt-ridden or rigid and pharisaical. So when we apply the Scriptures, we must make a distinction between the positive and negative commandments to know how to respond to them.

RULE EIGHT

Each person is individually responsible for applying the Scriptures to his or her own life.

Beginning with conversion, Christians are taught to function in the community of believers. Within this community, we are responsible for helping to monitor the behavior of our fellow Christians. The author of Hebrews says, for example: "Encourage one another daily, as long as it is called Today, so that none of you may be hardened by sin's deceitfulness" (Hebrews 3:13).

Paul says essentially the same thing to Timothy: "Preach the Word; be prepared in season and out of season; correct, rebuke and encourage—with great patience and careful instruction" (2 Timothy 4:2).

If the recalcitrant believer does not heed exhortation or rebuke, then the Christian community is to follow the method of discipline prescribed by Jesus in Matthew 18:15–19:

"If your brother sins against you, go and show him his fault, just between the two of you. If he listens to you, you have won your brother over. But if he will not listen, take one or two others along, so that 'every matter may be established by the testimony of two or three witnesses.' If he refuses to listen to them, tell it to the church; and if he refuses to listen even to the church, treat him as you would a pagan or a tax collector.

"I tell you the truth, whatever you bind on earth will be bound in heaven, and whatever you loose on earth will be loosed in heaven.

"Again, I tell you that if two of you on earth agree about anything you ask for, it will be done for you by my Father in heaven."

Community responsibility does not, however, absolve the individual of his or her own personal responsibility to apply the Scriptures. Most of the commands and admonitions in the Bible are given to the community, but their application is an individual responsibility. Sin may appear to be corporate when many people are transgressing God's commandments, but in the final analysis, it is always an individual problem in God's eyes.

Because no one likes to assume responsibility, society will always have those who shift responsibility for failure to someone else: Either the individual was improperly raised; society did not give him or her the "breaks" that were needed; or circumstances were such that the person *had* to behave wrongly.

Although this approach is attractive, because it absolves an individual of responsibility, it is unacceptable in the light of biblical teaching. Each person is responsible for applying the Scriptures to his or her own life. Failing to make application is a personal matter.

Paul, in writing to the Corinthians, warns: "For we must all appear before the judgment seat of Christ, that each one may receive what is due him for the things done while in the body, whether good or bad" (2 Corinthians 5:10).

Judgment is individual, not corporate. Each of us is responsible for applying the Scriptures to our lives, and each of us must give an account before God of how we have done.

RULE NINE

In all things, we must be teachable. We must be willing to admit that we are wrong, change direction, and appear inconsistent.

Nothing sticks in the throat of the proud believer like the need to admit that he or she is wrong: "It was the way I was raised," "I didn't really mean what I appeared to have said," "I've always believed this way, it's just that I didn't know how to say it."

We are ingenious in our ability to waltz around accountability. One of the most humorous illustrations of this is found in Exodus when Aaron made the golden calf: " 'Do not be angry, my Lord,' Aaron answered. 'You know how prone these people are to evil. They said to me, "Make us gods who will go before us. As for this fellow Moses who brought us up out of Egypt, we don't know what has happened to him." So I told them, "Whoever has any gold jewelry, take it off." Then they gave me the gold, and I threw it into the fire, and out came this calf!' " (Exodus 32:22–24).

The need to backtrack is not surprising and should not be embarrassing. All of us "see but a poor reflection," to use Paul's phrasing in 1 Corinthians 13:12. Only Jesus the Messiah was able to see clearly. John testifies in his gospel: "Jesus would not entrust himself to them, for he knew all men. He did not need man's testimony about man, for he knew what was in a man" (John 2:24–25).

Acts 9:1–9 is the record of Paul's conversion. Years later he reflects on it before King Agrippa. Here he discusses the implications of his encounter with Christ and says, "So then, King Agrippa, I was not disobedient to the vision from heaven. First to those in Damascus, then to those in Jerusalem and in all Judea, and to the Gentiles also, I preached that they should repent and turn to God and prove their repentance by their deeds" (Acts 26:19–20).

One day Paul is preaching that Christianity is a heresy, and he seeks with all he has to expunge it, and a week later he is preaching that Jesus is the Messiah, and Paul is expending his energies propagating the Gospel. Paul expresses his dramatic reversal beautifully: "They only heard the report: 'The man who formerly persecuted us is now preaching the faith he once tried to destroy' " (Galatians 1:23).

Ron, a close friend of ours, is sharp, articulate, a man of conviction. What he believes to be true he preaches unashamedly. But often he has found himself wrong. With no self-justification, no defense, he simply reverses himself and begins to preach what he now understands to be true. It is easy to see why people like this are a source of consternation to others.

Ghandi, the great spiritual and political leader of India, was not a Christian, but he had this characteristic. Often people saw him take one position only to find later that he had reversed himself. When challenged with inconsistency, he would simply reply, "I have more facts now than I did then."

Such people are a bewilderment to the insecure. Only those who understand who they are can display this kind of flexibility, yet it is foundational for the life committed to applying God's Word. We must be willing to admit we are wrong, change direction, and appear inconsistent.

RULE TEN

The acknowledgment of wrong must be followed by restitution when it is within our power.

Restitution is a key application principle. Confession is not sufficient when it is within our power to make right the wrong. Sadly, we are a generation of people who feel they can walk away from the consequences of wrong with scarcely a nod of acknowledgment. Society has nourished the idea of such "easy-outs" as bankruptcy laws and di-

vorce. Not only is commitment to covenants and obligations
lacking, but so also is the acknowledgment of sin followed by
restitution.

Psychology deals with guilt by placing the emphasis on the
symptom rather than the disease. But guilt can never be
abolished by dealing with guilt; it can only satisfactorily be
handled by dealing with the root problem—sin. People *feel* guilty
because they *are* guilty.

One of Jesus' claims that shook the religious community of His
day was the assertion that He could forgive sin. At the heart of
the Christian message is the assurance that forgiveness comes
through Christ's finished work. This forgiveness, however,
should be followed by restitution whenever possible. Jesus told
Zacchaeus, the dishonest tax collector in Luke 19: "Today
salvation has come to this house, because this man, too, is a son
of Abraham." What evoked such a response was not only
Zacchaeus' willingness to believe but also his willingness to
follow that belief with restitution: "Zacchaeus stood up and said
to the Lord, 'Look, Lord! Here and now I give half of my
possessions to the poor, and if I have cheated anybody out of
anything, I will pay back four times the amount' " (Luke 19:8).

This willingness to right wrongs is in keeping with John the
Baptist's ministry. He cried out to the people of his generation,
"Produce fruit in keeping with repentance" (Matthew 3:8).

At times restitution is impossible. Years ago I cheated a man
out of forty dollars. After I became a Christian, I sought in vain
to find him. Since I was unable to make it right with him, I gave
the forty dollars to the Lord's work.

Many times, however, restitution is possible. A good friend of
ours from Oklahoma City was forced into bankruptcy, leaving
behind a trail of debts. Although the law had absolved him of any
responsibility for repayment, he vowed before God to make it
right. After many years, every creditor was repaid, and his story
has become a testimony to other conscientious Christians who
understand their obligation to make restitution.

GROUP

# Principles on Our Perception of God's Word

**OUR PERCEPTION OF GOD'S WORD
IS VITAL FOR SUSTAINED AND
MEANINGFUL GROWTH IN
SCRIPTURAL APPLICATION.**

All the great men and women of the Bible were committed to the purity and holiness of the Word of God and to obedience to it. In his later years Daniel still studied the works of Jeremiah (Daniel 9), and he governed and controlled his life by what the Word of God instructed him to do. Christ was also committed to the holiness of the Bible: "Do not think that I have come to abolish the Law or the Prophets; I have not come to abolish them but to fulfill them. I tell you the truth, until heaven and earth disappear, not the smallest letter, not the least stroke of a pen, will by any means disappear from the Law until everything is accomplished.

Anyone who breaks one of the least of these commandments and teaches others to do the same will be called least in the kingdom of heaven, but whoever practices and teaches these commands will be called great in the kingdom of heaven" (Matthew 5:17–19).

The author of the book of Hebrews says that God's Word is alive and active, cutting more keenly than any double-edged sword (Hebrews 4:12). Such an attitude toward the Bible must be true of us also.

Principles 11–13 address key perceptions concerning the Word of God, concepts essential to the maturing process:

11. We must consider God's command rather than His chastisement as the motive for application.

12. Knowledge carries with it both privilege and responsibility.

13. There is no such thing as a nonessential command.

RULE ELEVEN

We must consider God's command rather than His chastisement as the motive for application.

About seventy guests had gathered at Jim's home for a discussion. Most were uncommitted and had come to this friendly, open environment to ask questions about God. As the discussion moved to whether a literal heaven and hell exist, Bob said, "I wish I could know for sure whether there is a hell. If there isn't, I wouldn't spend so much time trying to be good."

Like many, Bob works hard at "being good" out of fear that if he is bad, he will be the object of God's wrath. He is motivated by fear.

Love is a higher and more noble motive for application than fear. Such a motive causes a person to think, "I know that God is absolute purity and holiness. There is nothing false or evil about Him. Simply because He said it, His word is worthy of obedience. To do His will is best for all concerned."

Although most people agree that this is how we should respond, none of us can consistently execute these intentions. Not only do we frequently fail to meet God's expectations, but when we do meet them, it is often out of fear of His rod.

If, however, our gaze is fixed on what will happen to us if we fail to conform to His will, we will receive mixed signals. God's rebuke varies in intensity, and not just according to the size of the transgression. For reasons known only to Him, the severity of the chastisement and the seriousness of the infraction do not always seem to match.

In Exodus, Aaron, the high priest designate, makes an idol in the likeness of a golden calf. Although God is angry, Aaron apparently receives no punishment. Later, however, when Nadab and Abihu, the sons of Aaron, offer "unauthorized fire" before the Lord, they are destroyed. Aaron is told that if he weeps over their deaths, he too will be destroyed (Leviticus 10:1–7). Aaron makes an idol and nothing happens to him. But if he mourns his sons' deaths, God will kill him.

Exodus 2:11–12 narrates an incident in Moses' life: "One day, after Moses had grown up, he went out to where his own people were and watched them at their hard labor. He saw an Egyptian beating a Hebrew, one of his own people. Glancing this way and that and seeing no one, he killed the Egyptian and hid him in the sand." Another incident in the life of Moses demonstrates the seeming inconsistency of God's rebuke:

> The LORD said to Moses, "Take the staff, and you and your brother Aaron gather the assembly together. Speak to that rock before their eyes and it will pour out its water. You will bring water out of the rock for the community so they and their livestock can drink."
> So Moses took the staff from the LORD's presence, just as he commanded him. He and Aaron gathered the assembly together in

front of the rock and Moses said to them, "Listen, you rebels, must we bring you water out of this rock?" Then Moses raised his arm and struck the rock twice with his staff. Water gushed out, and the community and their livestock drank.

But the LORD said to Moses and Aaron, "Because you did not trust in me enough to honor me as holy in the sight of the Israelites, you will not bring this community into the land I give them" (Numbers 20:7–12).

Moses strikes a man dead, but God never calls him to account. He strikes a rock out of frustration over Israel's unbelief, and God says he can never enter into the promised land.

A man gathers sticks for a fire on the Sabbath, and the punishment is death (Numbers 5:32), while seemingly far greater infractions of God's law are recorded without severe consequences. If we look at retribution as a means of motivating us to obedience, we will be confused. Accountability to God is certain, but it cannot always be seen clearly. Our analysis of an act of disobedience is frequently different than God's. He warns: " 'For my thoughts are not your thoughts, neither are your ways my ways,' declares the LORD. 'As the heavens are higher than the earth, so are my ways higher than your ways and my thoughts than your thoughts' " (Isaiah 55:8–9).

God's accountability system appears to change but His commandments never change. We must consider the commands and that the Sovereign of the universe has asked us to keep them as the source of our motivation rather than fear of His retribution.

RULE TWELVE

Knowledge carries with it both privilege and responsibility.

Acquiring knowledge is both liberating and enjoyable. To understand truth, to come to grips with things as they are, to have one's mind broadened and expanded—these are some of the most pleasurable experiences that life affords. Conversely, to be ignorant is to live in bondage. Ignorant people are often guided by their superstitions and are open to exploitation by both man and the devil. People who have no desire or no opportunity to learn are bound in darkness.

The psalmist exalted: "Your word is a lamp to my feet and a light for my path" (Psalm 119:105). The Bible likens knowledge of God's Word to a light that reveals where a person is going; it "lights the path."

Another delightful aspect of knowledge involves the love two people have for one another. When I love others, I want to get to know them. I want to understand how they think, feel, and perceive reality. Such love lies at the very heart of the devotional life for the Christian. When an individual falls in love with Jesus Christ, he develops an insatiable appetite for knowing Him. Knowing all about a person is the natural by-product of loving that person.

An awesome responsibility, however, accompanies knowledge. Again and again, the Scriptures remind us that knowledge demands application. James pointed out that to hear or know the Word and to fail to apply it is to live in self-deception (James 1:22).

Nothing dismays God more than when we know and do not apply. Conversely, nothing delights God more than to see us apply what we know.

Matthew 13 records a series of parables that Jesus gave in His public ministry, all dealing with the kingdom of heaven. After the first one, the Parable of the Sower, the disciples asked:

"Why do you speak to the people in parables?"
He replied, "The knowledge of the secrets of the kingdom of heaven has been given to you, but not to them. Whoever has will be given more, and he will have an abundance. Whoever does not have, even what he has will be taken from him. This is why I speak to them in parables: 'Though seeing, they do not see; though hearing, they do

not hear or understand.' In them is fulfilled the prophecy of Isaiah: 'You will be ever hearing but never understanding; you will be ever seeing but never perceiving. For this people's heart has become calloused; they hardly hear with their ears, and they have closed their eyes. Otherwise they might see with their eyes, hear with their ears, understand with their hearts and turn, and I would heal them.' But blessed are your eyes because they see, and your ears because they hear. For I tell you the truth, many prophets and righteous men longed to see what you see but did not see it, and to hear what you hear but did not hear it.

"Listen then to what the parable of the sower means." (Matthew 13:10–18)

Jesus' answer is extraordinary. He says that He speaks in parables so that the people can hear but not understand.

The people to whom Jesus ministered had absorbed vast quantities of knowledge but were short on application. Jesus spoke in parables so that these people would fail to understand, simply because their mindset demonstrated a refusal to apply God's Word.

In formal education, knowledge and application are considered synonymous; testing is often intended to determine how much knowledge the students have retained. But no effort is made to discover how much of it the student is applying. Perhaps the nature of education eliminates any endeavor to evaluate application. Not so with the Scriptures; God insists that knowledge be followed by application. Knowledge is a wonderful and delightful privilege, but it is also a responsibility.

RULE THIRTEEN

There is no such thing as a nonessential command.

By definition, a command is essential; commandments are given to be obeyed. When we skirt them with fancy logic, such as "cultural context" or "unreasonableness," we do injustice to Scripture. The Pharisees ignored the commands and thereby provoked the ire of Jesus. The probing question of our Lord relates to us as well: "Why do you break the command of God for the sake of your tradition?" (Matthew 15:3).

If nonessential commands do exist, what is the standard or criteria for deciding which ones are essential and which are not? Even an objective evaluation would tend to make the decision on the basis of culture. Culture is an insidious impediment to application. Whenever we dismiss scriptural commands or teachings because of culture, it is the culture of our day rather than the culture of the Scriptures that causes us to come to such a conclusion. Increasingly the moral standards of the church are being eroded by the misconception that some commands are cultural and, therefore, nonessential. In some congregations "alternate lifestyles" are encouraged, including premarital sex and homosexuality. Some even argue for the ordination of homosexuals.

The problem is not culture. In the United States we find a generation of people who feel that the voice of authority is negotiable. In an editorial, *Time* magazine pointed out that disregard for the law is becoming epidemic. People feel free to transgress the vehicle codes, running red lights and stop signs, and disregarding rights of way. Flagrant abuse of drugs abounds, along with an utter disregard for the law. Young men feel that they can disregard with impunity the law that says they must register for the draft. Teachers feel that they have to function as policemen in the classroom rather than educators.

Writing to the Ephesians, Paul deals with the various roles of authority and our need to comply: "Children, obey your parents in the Lord, for this is right. 'Honor your father and mother'— which is the first commandment with a promise—'that it may go well with you and that you may enjoy long life on the earth' " (Ephesians 6:1–3).

The command is not for parents to make their children obey, but rather for children to obey and honor their parents. The responsibility is with the child, not the parent. If a child does not learn to respect the voice of authority, that disobedience has far-reaching ramifications. A child who does not learn to obey his parents will have a difficult time obeying teachers, the law of the land, and any voice of authority, including the Bible.

Imposed discipline builds self-discipline. If our children do not learn to obey and honor their parents, they grow up seeing no need for self-discipline. The good of the individual as that individual perceives it, rather than the good of the society, becomes paramount. The laws of God and the state are not to be obeyed; they are to be taken under advisement, evaluated in light of the person's own perception of his or her needs, and handled accordingly.

One young couple recently went through a divorce. She reasoned: "I know that the Bible says that I am not to divorce, but I also know that God loves me and has my best interests at heart. He wants me to be happy. We are not under law but under grace. Because God loves me and is gracious toward me, my happiness is more important than the law 'do not divorce.' I have tried to make the marriage work; I cannot. I am unhappy, and God would rather have me break the law and be happy than keep the law and be perpetually unhappy. Therefore, I feel that God would rather have me divorce than remain unhappily married."

As well-reasoned as this appears, it is predicated on the assumption that God's commandments and one's happiness are mutually exclusive. The insidiousness of such reasoning stems from concluding that all authority, irrespective of its origin, is negotiable. Such reasoning destroys the individual, the society, and the person's relationship with God. God views this as rebellion. Nothing provokes His ire more quickly. A person cannot have a heart for application and conclude that God's commandments are negotiable. There simply is no such thing as a nonessential command.

RULE FOURTEEN

We must not insist that we will obey only after a seeming contradiction in commandments is resolved.

Some commandments in the Bible seem to contradict one another. In Luke 14:26, for example, Jesus says we must hate our family and our own lives if we are to be disciples. But then Paul states in 1 Timothy 5:8 that if we do not provide for our families we have denied the faith and are worse than unbelievers.

One could easily conclude that these two statements are mutually exclusive concepts, for how can an individual do both? The temptation is to say, "Since Jesus' words are more authoritative that Paul's, I will obey Jesus rather than Paul." Or we may conclude that we will obey neither command until their apparent contradictions are resolved.

We cannot, however, allow seeming contradictions to paralyze us into inactivity. We must seek, rather, to obey the commands with equal zeal. I am my brother's keeper. My brothers, sisters, father, mother, wife, and children are my responsibility. If I do not provide for them, I am, as the apostle Paul says, "worse than an infidel."

On the other hand, my commitment to Christ is singularly unique above all other commitments that I have in life. Every relationship I have on earth pales in comparision to the significance of my relationship with Jesus Christ. In that sense, as a Christian, my loyalty and allegiance is first and foremost to Christ. Obedience to other authorities, including those in the family unit, must defer to Christ's authority.

In applying Scripture we must be careful not to insist on seeming contradictions to be resolved as a prerequiste for obedience.

13 Principles on the Product of Disobedience

NO MATTER WHAT THE RATIONALE FOR DISOBEDIENCE, DISOBEDIENCE ALWAYS LEADS TO BEING AT ODDS WITH GOD AND CONTRIBUTES TO OUR DEMISE.

The first three groups of principles in this book discuss preparing to apply God's Word and developing right attitudes to apply His word. Each principle affirms our positive responses to God. But to keep the picture in perspective, we must also understand the price to be paid for disobedience.

As the difficulty of becoming Christlike increases, we can easily rationalize adjusting God's commands. We begin to compromise morality an inch at a time. But we must always uphold God's law as the standard, not our opinion of the moment. If we are to err, we must err toward the Word, not toward our personal rationalizations and insights. Proverbs 3:5–6 exhorts: "Trust in the LORD with all your heart and lean not on your own understanding; in all your ways acknowledge him, and he will make your paths straight."

Disobedience only produces confusion and breaks down our relationship with God. Major principles regarding disobedience include:

15. Although there is no distinction between sins, there is a difference in consequences.

16. Disobedience adds to confusion when adverse circumstances come.

17. God's permissive will is entered only through a failure to apply the Scriptures.

18. We must refuse to yield to what we know is wrong. Satisfying the drive will only momentarily alleviate the hunger and will stimulate a desire for more.

19. "Culture" cannot serve as an excuse for not obeying God's commands.

20. The difference between a trial and a temptation lies in the response.

**RULE
FIFTEEN**

Although there is no distinction between sins, there is a difference in consequences.

In His teaching, Jesus presents sin as sin. There is no such thing as little sins and big sins. The distinction between venial and mortal sins is a human, not a biblical, distinction, for sin alienates a person from God, regardless of what type of sin it is.

For example, in Jesus' Sermon on the Mount, He said:

You have heard that it was said to the people long ago, "Do not murder, and anyone who murders will be subject to judgment." But I tell you that anyone who is angry with his brother will be subject to judgment. Again, anyone who says to his brother, "Raca," is answerable to the Sanhedrin. But anyone who says, "You fool!" will be in danger of the fire of hell. . . .

You have heard that it was said, "Do not commit adultery." But I tell you that anyone who looks at a woman lustfully has already committed adultery with her in his heart. . . .

You have heard that it was said, "Eye for eye, and tooth for tooth." But I tell you, Do not resist an evil person. If someone strikes you on the right cheek, turn to him the other also. (Matthew 5:21–22; 27–28; 38–39)

Jesus seems to suggest that the thought behind an act or the intent of an act are as bad as the act itself. He makes no distinctions between big and little sins.

Suppose I play golf. I stand on the first tee, hit the ball, and put a hook on it so that it leaves the golf course and goes through a huge window in a department store across the street. The manager comes out and says, "Who broke the window?" I respond, "Sir, I broke your window." He says, "That will cost you six thousand dollars." I counter, "Sir, I do not have six thousand dollars." He answers, "You broke the window, you pay." "How big was the golf ball?" I ask, and he answers by lifting his hand to show me the size. Pleased with where my argument is about to carry me, I suggest, "I put the ball through the window one time. I will buy you one piece of glass that big, and then we are even." His predictable response is, "No, you broke the window, you buy the whole window." We argue about it and go to court. Any objective jury would award the case to the manager.

God's law is like that plate-glass window. Some people put only a few holes in it, others put many holes in it. Some periodically put a hole here or there. Others destroy it with a howitzer. Still others seem to delight in jumping up and down on the pieces of broken glass until they grind them into sand. But one hole is all it takes; the window is broken, and the one who broke it is responsible for the purchase of the whole window.

In our relationship with God, as James said, "whoever keeps the whole law and yet stumbles at just one point is guilty of breaking all of it" (James 2:10). Sin is sin, and only one sin is necessary to require Jesus Christ's death on the cross in payment.

Although there is no distinction between sins, there is a difference in consequences. Jesus' words in Matthew 5:21–22 indicate that the consequences here on earth of my being angry at my brother are far different than the consequences if I kill him. In my mind, I can covet the money that is in the bank, and that is sin. If, however, I go the next step and rob the bank, the consequences of that act will be far more severe than coveting the money.

In all of life, a clear distinction must be maintained between how God views sin and the repercussions of that sin as they are expressed here on earth.

RULE SIXTEEN

Disobedience adds to confusion when adverse circumstances come.

Calamity is traumatic. When difficulties enter our lives, serious ones, such as death, disease, losing a job, or having a home destroyed by fire, the natural question to direct to God is "Why?" Why did the Lord allow these circumstances to happen?

The Bible reminds us that trials and tribulations come to all people— Christian and non-Christian alike. As a matter of fact, the Scriptures seem to suggest that Christians receive additional trials simply because we are identified with Christ and His sufferings. Peter writes: "Dear friends, do not be surprised at the painful trial you are suffering, as though something strange were happening to you. But rejoice that you participate in the sufferings of Christ, so that you may be overjoyed when his glory is revealed" (1 Peter 4:12–13).

There is another aspect of adverse circumstances, however, as the author of Hebrews reminds us:

> You have forgotten that word of encouragement that addresses you as sons: "My son, do not make light of the Lord's discipline, and do not lose heart when he rebukes you, because the Lord disciplines those he loves, and he punishes everyone he accepts as a son."
>
> Endure hardship as discipline; God is treating you as sons. For what son is not disciplined by his father? If you are not disciplined (and everyone undergoes discipline), then you are illegitimate children and not true sons. Moreover, we have all had human fathers who disciplined us and we respected them for it. How much more should we submit to the Father of our spirits and live! Our fathers disciplined us for a little while as they thought best; but God disciplines us for our good, that we may share in his holiness. No discipline seems pleasant at the time, but painful. Later on, however, it produces a harvest of righteousness and peace for those who have been trained by it. (Hebrews 12:5–11).

Here we are told that because the Lord loves us, He disciplines us. As His children, we can count on His chastening. He does not say that He punishes us; He merely corrects us. Punishment is given to achieve justice; chastisement is given to correct behavior. Our punishment has been borne by Christ on the cross. But when we err, we are chastened by the Lord.

"The law of the harvest" is different from chastisement; it is the natural reaping of what a person sows. Reaping may occur immediately after the transgression, or it may be postponed until the day of judgment, but the promise of the Scriptures is that all people will reap what they sow (Galatians 6:7).

When we live in willful disobedience to the Lord, and then calamity strikes, our spirit gives us unclear signals as to how we ought to evaluate the situation. We know that we all must go through trials and tribulations, but still we might be reaping God's chastisement, or we might be reaping what we have sown. Tragedy torments the guilty conscience when the believer has been living in disobedience to the Lord.

Such was the experience of Joseph's brothers. They sold Joseph into slavery. Years passed, and through a series of circumstances, Joseph became Egypt's prime minister. When famine hit Canaan, his brothers journeyed to Egypt to buy grain from the prime minister, not knowing that he was their brother. Before revealing himself to his brothers, Joseph tested them to see if they were still willing to betray one of their brothers. When the crisis developed, note what the brothers said to one another: "Surely we are being punished because of our brother. We saw how distressed he was when he pleaded with us for his life, but we would not listen; that's why this distress has come upon us" (Genesis 42:21).

The brothers had sinned, and they knew it. As a result, when adverse circumstances entered their lives, they were confused and could not understand what was taking place. Traumatic experiences will always be difficult, but they are further complicated when the believer lives in willful disobedience to the Lord.

RULE SEVENTEEN

God's permissive will is entered only through a failure to apply the Scriptures.

Nothing should terrify the believer so much as the thought of abiding in God's permissive will.

Israel's exodus from Egypt is filled with illustrations of what it means to live in His permissive will. The psalmist picks up this theme in Psalm 106: "They soon forgot his works; they waited not for his counsel: But lusted exceedingly in the wilderness, and tempted God in the desert. And

he gave them their request; but sent leanness into their souls"
(Psalm 106:13–15 KJV).

Similarly, the prophet Balaam did not consider God's Word to
be final. As Israel journeyed between Egypt and Canaan, they
made contact with the country of Moab. Balak, the Moabite
king, feared the Israelites and sought to have Balaam curse them.
Balak's ambassadors made a proposition to Balaam, who
talked it over with God. "God said to Balaam, 'Do not go with
them; you must not put a curse on those people, because they
are blessed' " (Numbers 22:12).

The answer was clear enough, and Balaam reported the
outcome to Balak's emissary: "The next morning Balaam got up
and said to Balak's princes, 'Go back to your own country, for
the LORD has refused to let me go with you' " (Numbers 22:13).

Refusing to take no for an answer, Balak returned to Balaam
who again asked the Lord. The Lord answered: " 'Since these
men have come to summon you, go with them, but do only what
I tell you.'

By the time we get to Numbers 24, we plainly see Balak's
stubbornness. He would have been wiser if he had asked Balaam
to *bless* Moab rather than *curse* Israel. But cursing Israel was all
he could think about.

Balaam obeyed the letter of God's law. He did not curse
Israel. But he did violate God's perfect will in refusing to view
Israel as special in God's sight. He suggested to Balak that if he
would cause the Moabites to sin sexually with the people of
Israel, God would curse the Hebrews. Moses writes: "They
were the ones who followed Balaam's advice and were the
means of turning the Israelites away from the LORD in what
happened at Peor, so that a plague struck the LORD's people"
(Numbers 31:16).

When God spoke to him, Balaam did not consider His Word
final. Balaam negotiated with God to get what he wanted. When
that failed, he sought by devious means to get his way. Three

times in the New Testament he is referred to as an evil man (2 Peter 2:15; Jude 11; Revelation 2:14).

Many people fear that they have entered into God's permissive will or received God's second best because of some decision they have made. Yet nothing in Scripture indicates that anybody enters into God's permissive will except through a flagrant violation of His known will.

Paul reminded Timothy: "God did not give us a spirit of timidity, but a spirit of power, of love and of self-discipline" (2 Timothy 1:7). Those who have a heart for application need not fear God's permissive will. The emphasis of our lives should not be on wondering whether we are in God's permissive will, but on living in obedience to what we understand to be His perfect will. Obedience is always the issue.

When God speaks, we must not argue. If we do, we may get what we want, but He will "send leanness" to our soul. God's permissive will is not an attractive place.

RULE EIGHTEEN

We must refuse to yield to what we know is wrong. Satisfying the drive will only momentarily alleviate the hunger and will stimulate a desire for more.

The Bible speaks a great deal about making no provision for the flesh. Paul, writing to the churches of Galatia, reminded them that "those who belong to Christ Jesus have crucified the sinful nature with its passions and desires" (Galatians 5:24). To the Romans he wrote: "So then, the law is holy, and the commandment is holy, righteous and good.

"Did that which is good, then, become death to me? By no means! But in order that sin might be recognized as sin, it produced death in me through what was good, so that through the commandment sin might become utterly sinful" (Romans 7:12–13).

Later he said: "And do not think about how to gratify the desires of the sinful nature" (Romans 13:14). Appetites and drives are God-given and are, therefore, good. But God does establish boundaries. When we exceed those boundaries under the pretext that it is "natural," not only are His commandments broken, but one's own life is also put in jeopardy.

Sex is a perfect example. Yielding to the drive does not lessen its urge; it only offers momentary relief. Satisfaction merely feeds the urge, and the desire for continued fulfillment increases. Like a boiler building a head of steam, each act increases the passion.

Marriage is the biblical norm for sexual fulfillment. When sex is practiced outside of marriage, guilt is incurred; the desire for continued fulfillment increases; and the willingness to yield grows with each transgression.

Commitment to the fulfillment of our appetites produces a vicious cycle. One experience, no matter how exotic, can never satisfy us. We always crave more, both qualitatively and quantitatively. In the quest for fulfillment, we search for larger and greener pastures.

A friend of ours changes jobs every two or three years. Once he has mastered a job, it loses its attractiveness; he becomes bored. His restless spirit looks elsewhere for a richer experience. This is the result of a life committed to fulfillment. Commitment must be to God's perfect will, never to self-gratification. We must be committed to a conviction rather than to a fulfilling experience.

If marriage is based on the meeting of my personal needs rather than commitment to my God-given partner, before long the marriage will show signs of stress. Marriage can, of course, be a perpetually fulfilling, even exotic, experience where my needs are met. But fulfillment is a by-product of commitment. To concentrate on our needs is to concentrate on the insatiable. A well-known casanova of our day is currently undergoing treatment for impotence. His condition may appear ludicrous, but it illustrates the sad plight of those who live for their own fulfillment.

An unused limb of the body will atrophy; use makes it strong. Similarly, human drives that are unbiblical or impossible to fulfill in a scriptural manner can best be controlled by starvation. Feeding them does not alleviate the hunger but only stimulates a desire for more. Abstinence causes the drive to atrophy.

RULE NINETEEN

Culture cannot serve as an excuse for not obeying God's commands.

When we consider the difference between American culture and Oriental society, we see certain principles in action. It is possible, for example, for one person to consider "good food" what another considers inedible. Convictions in these matters are greatly influenced by the experiences that make up a person's culture. Truth is not relative, but our ability to see truth is hindered by a world view that is a product of our culture.

Every generation needs to sort through its convictions to determine which are biblically based and which are based on culture. This must be done in two areas: First, and most easily discerned, are the prohibitions not biblically based, such as gambling and the use of alcohol. Although the believer is free to do those things not prohibited in the Bible, we are wise to think through why we believe what we believe.

Second, and possibly more subtle, are the biblical commands that we ignore because of the pressure of our culture. In Paul's letter to the Corinthians he said:

If any of you has a dispute with another, dare he take it before the ungodly for judgment instead of before the saints? Do you not know that the saints will judge the world? And if you are to judge the world, are you not competent to judge trivial cases? Do you not know that we will judge angels? How much more the things of this life! Therefore, if you have disputes about such matters, appoint as judges even men of little account in the church! I say this to shame you. Is it possible that there is nobody among you wise enough to judge a dispute between believers? But instead, one brother goes to law against another—and this in front of unbelievers!

The very fact that you have lawsuits among you means you have been completely defeated already. Why not rather be wronged? Why not rather be cheated? Instead, you yourselves cheat and do wrong, and you do this to your brothers" (1 Corinthians 6:1–8).

The passage denies a believer the right to take a fellow Christian to court. Yet the command is virtually ignored because our culture expects such matters to be settled in the courts rather than in the church. The excuse for such disobedience is a common one: In our culture the church is fragmented. Because we don't present a unified front, a believer can walk away from the authority of his church when displeased and go elsewhere.

In Sweden a large segment of the church condones premarital sex. It is an "accepted" practice. Is it possible that in a few years the church in the United States will follow Sweden's lead regarding premarital sex?

Society exerts great pressure on people to conform to its norms; yet not all that culture teaches is wrong. Culture is a mixture of iron and clay; much of what it teaches is good, but certainly not all. On one hand, God has used culture from the time of creation; on the other hand, we are urged not to allow it to "squeeze us into its mold" (Romans 12:2 PHILLIPS).

Whenever we are told that a biblical command need not be obeyed because it was cultural in its original context, and our culture is different from theirs, we should suspect that *our* culture, not the culture of Bible days, is the issue. It is not the cultural context of the Scriptures, but the cultural context of the believer that pressures him into not applying biblical teachings.

The Scriptures, along with their commands, transcend time and culture. Therefore, we must not allow culture to serve as an excuse for not obeying God's commands.

RULE TWENTY

The difference between a trial and a tempta- tion lies in the response.

In the New Testament there are two words that are used for our English words "tried," "tempted," "tempta- tion," "tested," and "trial." The first, *peira,* is used in passages such as Matthew 4:1; Mark 1:12–13; 1 Corinthians 10:13; James 1:12–14; and Hebrews 11:17, 36.

Hebrews 11:17 says: "By faith Abraham, when God tested him, offered Isaac as a sacrifice. He who had received the promises was about to sacrifice his one and only son." This verse refers to Genesis 22 where God called on Abraham to offer his son Isaac on Mount Moriah. Hebrews 11:17 tells us that God tried or tested Abraham to see if his faith was strong enough to obey.

James, however, makes an interesting observation: "Blessed is the man who perseveres under trial, because when he has stood the test, he will receive the crown of life that God has promised to those who love him.

"When tempted, no one should say, 'God is tempting me.' For God cannot be tempted by evil, nor does he tempt anyone; but each one is tempted when, by his own evil desire, he is dragged away and enticed" (James 1:12–14).

The word for "temptation" in James is the same word used for "tried" in Hebrews 11:17—*peira.* Yet James 1:13 says: "God cannot be tempted by evil, nor does he tempt anyone." At first this seems to be a contradiction, but James implies that although God *tests* the believer, He does not *tempt* him in the sense that He seeks his downfall. God's motive is never the believer's demise but the strengthening of faith and character.

When a trial or temptation comes into the believer's life, if it is handled properly, it can serve to his or her advantage. If the believer yields to temptation or succumbs to unbelief, then it works to his or her disadvantage.

In Job's life, we see an apparent contradiction. Job 2:3 says: "Then the LORD said to Satan, 'Have you considered my servant Job? There is no one on earth like him; he is blameless and upright, a man who fears God and shuns evil. And he still maintains his integrity, though you incited me against him to ruin him without any reason.' " Later, Job 2:7 says: "So Satan went out from the presence of the LORD and afflicted Job with painful sores from the soles of his feet to the top of his head."

Verse 3 says that God afflicted Job; verse 7 says Satan did the afflicting. Because God is sovereign and in control, and in His providence does not allow anything to touch the believer without His divine permission, no real distinction exists between the two. As Paul says: "No temptation has seized you except what is common to man. And God is faithful; he will not let you be tempted beyond what you can bear. But when you are tempted, he will also provide a way out so that you can stand up under it" (1 Corinthians 10:13).

God does not allow testing and temptation to come into a believer's life that exceeds his or her ability to overcome them; every trial and temptation includes the power to overcome. In the overcoming process the believer is strengthened.

Jesus is an illustration of this truth: "Then Jesus was led by the Spirit into the desert to be tempted by the devil" (Matthew 4:1). The Holy Spirit leads Jesus into the wilderness to be tempted by the devil, for through testing one discovers one's convictions.

The second word used in the New Testament for "tried," "trial," "temptation," and "tempted" is *dokime*. It is used in James 1:12 and in 1 Peter 1:7 and 4:12. It means "an object that is tested to prove its genuine value; certified; tested and proved worthy." 1 Peter 1:7 says that our faith is of greater worth than gold, the most valuable commodity on earth. In almost every generation gold has stood as the standard of value. The more uncertainty there is in the currency of a country, the more the people tend to invest in gold which does not lose its value.

God never brings trials and testings into our lives to cause us to fall into sin. According to Peter, the "trying of our faith" actually works to our advantage; the sufferings and difficulties encountered in the world establish that our faith is real, valuable, and certified as pure. Regardless of its source, the difference between a trial and a temptation lies in our response to it.

Principles on The Life of Application

PART 1:
WE CANNOT MEASURE PROGRESS IN APPLICATION.

Measurement is an important concept in our society; it is the foundation of worth and accomplishment. Through measurement, we make long-range projections and establish goals; without it we do not know how far we have gone, and we have a difficult time planning for the future.

Without it, control is impossible. If a company cannot measure the quantity and quality of its product, it cannot control its future. Not to measure is to be out of control, and to be out of control is to be insecure.

Every individual has a built-in desire to control. We want to control our environment, our destiny—in short, the world in which we live. Many people refuse to become Christians out of a fear that they will lose control of their lives.

A superficial analysis, however, reveals our lack of control. None of us determines such things as our sex, appearance, nationality, era of history, color of skin, size, gifts and abilities, longevity, or circumstances. What we do control is our response to those things over which we have no control.

When we are out of control, we are dependent. When we are in control, we are independent. Control is at the very heart of our relationship to God. He wants us to be dependent, walking by faith. Because measurement is essential for control, it can be a problem in striving for dependence and faith.

We can measure the quantitative aspects of the Christian life— the number of days a person has private devotions, the frequency of church attendance, the number of people to whom one witnesses. But the qualitative dimension of the Christian life is, for the most part, unmeasurable. The time a person spends in prayer is measurable; the quality of that prayer is not.

The characteristics of Christlikeness defy measurement, such as the fruit of the Spirit: "love, joy, peace, patience, kindness, goodness, faithfulness, gentleness and self-control" (Galatians 5:22). Lordship is qualitative; so are patience, humility, and a host of other virtues. God has designed the Christian life so that the qualities that are important in God's economy can only be attained by maintaining a posture of dependence and faith.

Measurement should not be confused with evaluation. We evaluate all that comes into our lives. But measurement implies a standard; a person reaches the standard or does not quite measure up. Evaluation has no standard; it is comparative.

Janice is a Christian disciple. We cannot measure her walk with God—unless by the standard of perfection (Matthew 5:48), in which case she, like everyone else, falls short. On the other hand, we can evaluate Janice by comparing where she is today with where she was a year ago.

We must resist the temptation to measure. We cannot look to people and circumstances for feedback in our growth, nor must we measure the growth of others.

21. Circumstances do not indicate God's approval or disapproval.

22. The validity of personal application is not dependent on another's acceptance or approval.

23. We must resist the temptation to judge others as less spiritual when they do what the Lord has forbidden us to do.

RULE TWENTY-ONE

Circumstances do not indicate God's approval or disapproval.

God in His providence allows circumstances to enter our lives. They may heighten our awareness of the need for application, but they are poor indicators of God's approval or disapproval. We view most of our circumstances as either negative or positive, but our perception of them is not always the same as God's.

We tend to be experience-oriented, or feeling-oriented; circumstances are construed to be either good or bad depending on how we feel. If the circumstance is positive, making me feel good, I conclude that God loves me. On the other hand, if the circumstance is negative, making me unhappy, I conclude that God is either angry with me or does not care.

Using circumstances as a barometer of God's pleasure or displeasure is not new. The psalmist wrestled with the same problem; in Psalm 73 he expresses dismay over the triumph of wicked men. The psalmist, in contrast, seems to have kept God's law in vain. He struggles with the contradiction, finding himself envying the prosperity of the wicked until God reveals to him the ultimate outcome: "When I tried to understand all this, it was oppressive to me till I entered the sanctuary of God; then I understood their final destiny" (Psalm 73:16–17).

The writer undergoes a transformation in his thinking, but not through anything he saw or experienced. His conclusion was derived through faith. His hope was based on God's promises.

Experience tells us that the righteous do not always prosper. Frequently the wicked prosper and oppress the righteous. Clearly, we cannot depend on circumstances to indicate God's approval or disapproval.

As Job's three friends sought to evaluate his predicament, they reasoned that because God blesses the righteous and punishes the wicked, Job's adverse circumstances were an indication of God's displeasure. If Job would but repent, God would bless him. Yet in Job 2:3 God says that he had destroyed Job "without any reason," which means the calamity that befell Job was not a product of Job's sin or unrighteousness. His circumstances, like ours, could not be interpreted as an indicator of God's approval or disapproval.

RULE TWENTY-TWO

The validity of personal application is not dependent on another's acceptance or approval.

People often view applying God's Word as a risk because the Scriptures appear illogical—the Bible calls on us to do things that the world considers foolish. For example, Jesus said: "If anyone would come after me, he must deny himself and take up his cross daily and follow me. For whoever wants to save his life will lose it, but whoever loses his life for me will save it" (Luke 9:23–24).

In Mark 10:31 Jesus said that those who wish to be first must be last; in Luke 6:38, He suggested that the secret to getting is giving.

If we evaluate such truths from the world's perspective, they appear to be nonsense. When we try to put them into practice in our lives, we can count on a certain amount of disapproval.

Little of what Abraham did in obedience to God would have gained approval from the people of his—or any—generation: "By faith Abraham, when called to go to a place he would later receive as his inheritance, obeyed and went, even though he did not know where he was going" (Hebrews 11:8).

If he were alive today, Abraham would arrive at the office some Monday morning and announce his plans to quit. When asked why, he would answer that he was leaving town. As people asked where he was going, his answer according to this verse would be, "I don't know." We can imagine the approval we would gain for such a plan—quitting our jobs, selling our homes, leaving town without any idea where we were going.

Years later when Abraham is in the Promised Land of Canaan, God comes to him again: "Take your son, your only son, Isaac, whom you love, and go to the region of Moriah. Sacrifice him there as a burnt offering on one of the mountains I will tell you about" (Genesis 22:2). If God were to ask me to take my only child and offer him as a sacrifice, how many people would I find who would approve or accept? No doubt if Abraham had sought counsel on this command from God, the vote would have been unanimously in favor of not offering Isaac.

Those who love us most are often the strongest in their objections to our obeying "illogical" commands. They do not want us to disobey God, but they also do not want us to suffer or do foolish things. When the Bible says that we are to be crucified with Christ (Galatians 2:20), we cannot expect universal acceptance or approval when we seek to obey. A command's validity, or the application of any Scripture, for that matter, is not determined by another person's acceptance or approval.

RULE TWENTY-THREE

We must resist the temptation to judge others as less spiritual when they do what the Lord has forbidden us to do.

Because it is so easy to forget, we must constantly remind ourselves that application is simply responding properly to what God says. The process of sanctification is different in each person's life. The common core of application that we all share is the standard expressed in the absolute commandments of the Bible. Our culture, however, prohibits certain activities that the Bible does not say are wrong, such as smoking, drinking, and gambling.

Among the extra-biblical prohibitions found in the Mormon Church, for instance, is the drinking of beverages containing caffeine. The Mormons borrowed this, along with a host of other extra-biblical prohibitions, from evangelical Christianity a century or so ago. Most evangelical Christians have dropped the prohibition; the Mormons have not.

Because we are each in a different place in the application process, we cannot judge those whose convictions differ from our own. J. Gresham Machen, the founding president of Westminster Seminary, once said, "When the church forbids what God allows; it soon allows what God forbids."

Paul gives us a proper perspective on judging in his first epistle to the Corinthians and in his letter to the Colossians. First Corinthians 4:3–5 says: "I care very little if I am judged by you or by any human court; indeed, I do not even judge myself. My conscience is clear, but that does not make me innocent. It is the Lord who judges me. Therefore judge nothing before the appointed time; wait till the Lord comes. He will bring to light what is hidden in darkness and will expose the motives of men's hearts. At that time each will receive his praise from God."

Paul reminds the Corinthians that he does not even know his

own motives, much less those of another. We cannot, therefore, judge one another's motives. First Corinthians 5:1–5 contrasts this principle with another kind of judging: "It is actually reported that there is sexual immorality among you, and of a kind that does not occur even among pagans: A man has his father's wife. And you are proud! Shouldn't you rather have been filled with grief and have put out of your fellowship the man who did this? Even though I am not physically present, I am with you in spirit. And I have already passed judgment on the one who did this, just as if I was present. When you are assembled in the name of our Lord Jesus and I am with you in spirit, and the power of our Lord Jesus is present, hand this man over to Satan, so that the sinful nature may be destroyed and his spirit saved on the day of the Lord."

Paul is talking about the transgression of a negative commandment: one of the Corinthians is having an incestuous relationship with his father's wife. This kind of behavior must be judged by the Christian community.

In Colossians 2:16–17 Paul talks about a third kind of judging: "Therefore do not let anyone judge you by what you eat or drink, or with regard to a religious festival, a New Moon celebration or a Sabbath day. These are a shadow of the things that were to come; the reality, however, is found in Christ."

In this passage Paul refers to activities that are not prohibited in the Scriptures but may be avoided by certain Christians out of personal conviction. He says, in essence, that we cannot judge those who do what our personal convictions forbid us to do. We must resist the temptation to judge others as less spiritual than us when they do the things the Lord has forbidden us to do.

PART 2:
THE OBJECTIVES OF APPLYING
GOD'S WORD TO OUR LIVES ARE TO
PLEASE GOD, TO STRIVE FOR
MORAL EXCELLENCE, AND TO
LEAVE A GODLY LEGACY.

God speaks of these three major products of obedience. They are discussed in rules 1, 24, and 25. Rather than attempting to measure the results of application, we must learn to wait and view the product of our commitment to the Word of God and its application from God's perspective. God's promised results are exciting but not quantitative. His feedback comes to us in ways that bring joy but exclude measurement. If we commit our tasks to Him, we receive His pleasure, moral excellence, and a positive impact on posterity.

1. Application must be focused on pleasing God rather than pleasing others.

24. The path to intellectual excellence is curiosity, investigation, and experimentation, but the path to moral excellence is obedience.

25. Our conduct, good or bad, will affect the generations to follow.

RULE TWENTY-FOUR

The path to intellectual excellence is curiosity, investigation, and experimentation; but the path to moral excellence is obedience.[1]

Risk taking, or faith, is at the heart of the believer's life, but the risk is always toward being moral, never toward being immoral. Nowhere in the Scriptures do we find believers admonished to indulge in acts of immorality to gain knowledge. As a matter of fact, we find just the opposite: "Everyone had heard about your obedience so I am full of joy over you; but I want you to be wise about what is good, and innocent about what is evil" (Romans 16:19).

The word "innocent" connotes being half-witted regarding evil; that is, there is no need for the believer to know all there is to know about unrighteous matters.

Paul reiterates the same idea in 1 Corinthians 14:20: "Brothers, stop thinking like children. In regard to evil be infants, but in your thinking be adults."

In understanding life, the apostle encourages us to understand as adults, with one exception—in evil matters. In this area we are to be as children, naïve and innocent.

Our permissive age teaches us to experiment in moral matters as one would experiment in scientific matters: "Try it! You don't know what it's like until you do it." We are encouraged to experiment with sex, drugs, and trial marriages. Even if such experimentation leads an individual to Christ, such a conversion comes at the cost of moral bankruptcy. Experimentation can never lead a person to moral excellence.

From a biblical perspective, the path to moral excellence is always obedience. Paul says in Colossians 3:5–10: "Put to death, therefore, whatever belongs to your earthly nature: sexual

---

[1] Chambers, Oswald, *Shade of His Hand.*

immorality, impurity, lust, evil desires and greed, which is idolatry. Because of these, the wrath of God is coming. You used to walk in these ways, in the life you once lived. But now you must rid yourselves of all such things as these: anger, rage, malice, slander, and filthy language from your lips. Do not lie to each other, since you have taken off your old self with its practices and have put on the new self, which is being renewed in knowledge in the image of its Creator.''

The scientific method is appropriate in amoral matters where scriptural commands are not at stake. But to treat the moral realm as one would treat the scientific realm is to lead to degradation and depravity. When psychology and psychiatry encourage using the scientific method in moral areas, such application can lead to nothing but personal ruin.

RULE TWENTY-FIVE

Our conduct, good or bad, will affect the generations to follow.

This theme is repeated throughout the Scriptures. When we do well, our children reap the benefits. When we do evil, our children suffer the consequences. This truth can be seen by observation as well as learned through Scripture.

As the children of Israel were making their exodus from Egypt, en route to Mount Sinai, they were hindered by the Amalekites who fought them at Rephidim: "The Lord said to Moses, 'Write this on a scroll as something to be remembered and make sure that Joshua hears it, because I will completely blot out the memory of Amalek from under heaven.'

"Moses built an altar and called it The Lord is my Banner. He said, 'For hands were lifted up to the throne of the Lord. The Lord will be at war against the Amalekites from generation to generation'' (Exodus 17:14–16).

Hundreds of years later God instructed the prophet Samuel to have King Saul fulfill this vow: "Samuel said to Saul, 'I am the one the LORD sent to anoint you king over his people Israel; so listen now to the message from the LORD. This is what the LORD Almighty says: "I will punish the Amalekites for what they did to Israel when they waylaid them as they came up from Egypt. Now go, attack the Amalekites and totally destroy everything that belongs to them. Do not spare them; put to death men and women, children and infants, cattle and sheep, camels and donkeys"'" (1 Samuel 15:1–3).

The Amalekites were destroyed even though the generation that died did no wrong to Israel. Their forefathers, hundreds of years before, provoked God's wrath.

God reminded the prophet Ezekiel: "The soul who sins is the one who will die. The son will not share the guilt of the father, nor will the father share the guilt of the son. The righteousness of the righteous man will be credited to him and the wickedness of the wicked will be charged against him" (Ezekiel 18:20).

Each person is responsible for his or her own sin; the father does not bear responsibility for the son's sin, nor does the son bear responsibility for the father's sin. Nevertheless, the consequences of one's sin linger and are inherited by future generations, just as the blessings of one person or family linger and are inherited by future generations.

Isaac is an illustration of a person who is blessed because of his father's faithfulness. The Lord reaffirmed His covenant with Isaac, appearing to him with the words: "I am the God of your father Abraham. Do not be afraid, for I am with you; I will bless you and will increase the number of your descendants for the sake of my servant Abraham" (Genesis 26:24). Isaac was promised blessing because of Abraham's relationship with God.

A man's sin also affects his progeny. A man of God comes to Eli, the high priest of Israel, rebuking him for his failure to raise his sons properly: "Therefore the LORD, the God of Israel, declares: 'I promised that your house and your father's house would minister before me forever.' But now the LORD declares: 'Far be it from me! Those who honor me I will honor, but those who despise me will be disdained. The time is coming when I will cut short your strength and the strength of your father's house, so that there will not be an old man in your family line and you will see distress in my dwelling. Although good will be done to Israel, in your family line there will never be an old man. Every one of you that I do not cut off from my altar will be spared only to blind your eyes with tears and grieve your heart, and all your descendants will die in the prime of life" (1 Samuel 2:30–33). Because of Eli's failure, he is told twice, "There will not be an old man in your family line."

In contrast, an evil man, because of his forefathers' righteousness, does not receive fully what he deserves. Concerning Abijah, son of Rehoboam, it is written: "He committed all the sins his father had done before him; his heart was not fully devoted to the LORD his God, as the heart of David his forefather had been. Nevertheless, for David's sake the LORD his God gave him a lamp in Jerusalem by raising up a son to succeed him and by making Jerusalem strong. For David had done what was right in the eyes of the LORD and had not failed to keep any of the LORD's commands all the days of his life—except in the case of Uriah the Hittite" (1 Kings 15:3–5).

Abijah committed all the sins his father Rehoboam did. Yet God said that for David's sake He would not utterly destroy his lineage. David's faithfulness affected the generations that followed.

In 1 Kings 14:6–14, the infant son of Jeroboam was ill, and Jeroboam sent his wife to inquire from the prophet, Ahijah, what would happen:

> So when Ahijah heard the sound of her footsteps at the door, he said, "Come in, wife of Jeroboam. Why this pretense? I have been sent to you with bad news. Go, tell Jeroboam that this is what the LORD, the God of Israel, says: 'I raised you up from among the people

and made you a leader over my people Israel. I tore the kingdom away from the house of David and gave it to you, but you have not been like my servant David, who kept my commands and followed me with all his heart, doing only what was right in my eyes. You have done more evil than all who lived before you. You have made for yourself other gods, idols made of metals; you have provoked me to anger and thrust me behind your back.

" 'Because of this I am going to bring disaster on the house of Jeroboam. I will cut off from Jeroboam every last male in Israel— slave or free. I will burn up the house of Jeroboam as one burns dung, until it is all gone. Dogs will eat those belonging to Jeroboam who die in the city, and the birds of the air will feed on those who die in the country. The LORD has spoken!' "

"As for you, go back home. When you set foot in your city, the boy will die. All Israel will mourn for him and bury him. He is the only one belonging to Jeroboam who will be buried, because he is the only one in the house of Jeroboam in whom the LORD, the God of Israel, has found anything good.

"The LORD will raise up for himself a king over Israel who will cut off the family of Jeroboam." (1 Kings 14:6–14)

Three principles emerge from this passage: (1) What a person does appreciably affects his progeny (v. 10). (2) Children generally repeat their fathers' sins. The one who does not still dies early, yet remains in the grace of God (v. 13). (3) Many events in life are worse than death. From a biblical perspective, death is not a disaster, as verse 13 indicates. Life, therefore, must not be focused toward living but rather toward being the Lord's obedient servant.

This truth can be observed in everyday life. Scientists tell us that if we abuse our bodies with drugs, alcohol, tobacco, and other harmful substances, we affect the physical well-being of our children. Conversely, if parents work hard, discipline themselves, live moral, exemplary lives, gain fine reputations in the community, and excel in what they do, their children profit.

This principle began with Adam's and Eve's sin in the Garden of Eden. The suffering of humanity for thousands of years is the direct consequence of their sin. Plus people in every age have emulated Adam and Eve by living disobediently.

In every age people argue that there is no cause-and-effect relationship between what a person does today and what happens years later. God's word to Moses should sober us: "You shall not bow down to them or worship them; for I, the LORD your God, am a jealous God, punishing the children for the sins of the fathers to the third and the fourth generation of those who hate me" (Exodus 20:5).

Moses, prayed in Psalm 90:12: "Teach us to number our days aright, that we may gain a heart of wisdom." He understood the responsibility of continuity. Wise people have an appreciation for the process that brought them to where they are and sense their responsibility to the future.

15 Principles on People in the Process of Application

GOD USES PEOPLE TO HELP US GROW.

Community is an important part of the Christian life. Christ designed His Body in such a way that "maverick" existence is impossible. In 1 Corinthians 12–14, for example, we learn that the distribution of spiritual gifts insures that everyone has some gift and no one has all. The gifts that I have that the rest of the Body does not have make me important; the gifts that the Body has that I do not have make me dependent.

The importance of community is highlighted in Hebrews 10:24–25: "Let us consider how we may spur one another on toward love and good deeds. Let us not give up meeting together, as some are in the habit of doing, but let us encourage one another—and all the more as you see the Day approaching."

People have a powerful influence on each other's lives, either for better or for worse. The apostle John warns of the need to avoid negative influence: "If any one comes to you and does not bring this teaching, do not take him into your house or welcome him" (2 John 10).

By and large, however, fellowship with like-minded believers has a positive impact. We become like the people with whom we associate; if we want to be godly, we need to associate with godly people. Our fellow Christians influence us in specific ways.

26. We must maintain an accountability relationship with a group of people who will exhort us to faith and good works.

27. Godly counsel is helpful in the quest for obedience, but it should never be used to avoid personal responsibility.

> ## RULE TWENTY-SIX
>
> **We must maintain an accountability relationship with a group of people who will exhort us to faith and good works.**

The focus of application must be to please God rather than others (Rule 1). As important as this truth is, the balancing truth must also be remembered—we need people who love us enough to tell us when we are wrong and call us to account.

The Scriptures are full of admonitions and illustrations of accountability. Hebrews 3:13 admonishes us to "encourage one another daily, as long as it is called Today, so that none of you may be hardened by sin's deceitfulness."

Jesus laid down the procedure we are to follow when a brother falls into sin: "If your brother sins against you, go and show him his fault, just between the two of you. If he listens to you, you have won your brother over. But if he will not listen, take one or two others along, so that 'every matter may be established by the testimony of two or three witnesses.' If he refuses to listen to them, tell it to the church; and if he refuses to listen even to the church, treat him as you would a pagan or a tax collector" (Matthew 18:15–17).

In 2 Samuel 12 Nathan the prophet rebuked David. David with an amazing spirit of submission, responded to Nathan's charge: "I have sinned against the LORD" (2 Samuel 12:13). We should have such an attitude as we stand accountable to our brothers and sisters in the faith.

Not all accountability, of course, comes as rebuke. Often it is counsel: "The purposes of a man's heart are deep waters, but a man of understanding draws them out" (Proverbs 20:5). Other times it is encouragement: "Saul's son Jonathan went to David at Horesh and helped him find strength in God" (1 Samuel 23:16).

All believers need this kind of support. Jeremiah the prophet reminds us that "the heart is deceitful above all things and beyond cure" (Jeremiah 17:9). Accountability to other believers gives us objectivity and reduces our chances of deceiving ourselves.

We will do in front of God what we would never do in front of people. We will think thoughts and do deeds in God's presence that we would be ashamed of doing in the presence of people. So also, we will do in the presence of strangers what we won't do before friends.

The support group, therefore, functions as a check in our lives. Its very presence prods us toward righteousness. The writer of Hebrews exhorted: "Obey your leaders and submit to their authority. They keep watch over you as men who must give an account. Obey them so that their work will be a joy, not a burden, for that would be of no advantage to you" (Hebrews 13:17).

Many will find this support in their local congregation. Other churches are so large that support must be found in the Sunday-school class or some small informal group. Whatever the source, the component parts are counsel, support, rebuke when necessary, and a willingness to uphold one another in prayer. Such accountability is rooted in a loving, caring concern for one another.

RULE TWENTY-SEVEN

Godly counsel is helpful in the quest for obedience, but it should never be used to avoid personal responsibility.

In Jesus' ministry, he repeatedly emphasized to His disciples their need to walk by faith.

Faith plays a strategic role in the application process. Because application involves doing what we "know" God wants us to do, and because we cannot "know" in the scientific sense, we therefore must walk by faith as we apply the Scriptures.

In trying to minimize the risk, if not entirely eliminate it, we use godly counsel. But counsel can never be used to answer the question, "What should I do?" None of us can avoid the personal responsibility of trusting God in the application process.

What is the purpose of godly counsel? It can accomplish two things for the person who has an obedient heart. First, it can help us check the validity of our thinking. Some of us do not always think straight as we try to sort out how to respond to what we feel God wants us to do. Counsel can help us in that sorting process. Second, counsel can help us gain additional or new insights. As we wrestle with a decision, we may easily overlook certain truths that can be identified by people who take a fresh and objective view of our situation.

Judges 7 records God's deliverance of the children of Israel from the hand of the Midianites. As Gideon sought to obey God, he recognized the risk involved in facing the Midianite hoards.

He used a fleece to help affirm in his own heart that God was really leading him:

> Gideon said to God, "If you will save Israel by my hand as you have promised—look, I will place a wool fleece on the threshing floor. If there is dew only on the fleece and all the ground is dry, then I will know that you will save Israel by my hand, as you said." And that is what happened. Gideon rose early next day; he squeezed the fleece and wrung out the dew—a bowlful of water.
> Then Gideon said to God, "Do not be angry with me. Let me make just one more request. Allow me one more test with the fleece. This time make the fleece dry and the ground covered with dew." That night God did so. Only the fleece was dry; all the ground was covered with dew. (Judges 6:36–40)

The Bible does not prohibit a person from using a "fleece" to decide what he or she ought to do. The fleece, however, does not eliminate the need to walk by faith, it simply shifts the risk taking to a more objective form.

Counsel differs from authority in that all of us are under authority, and authority is to be obeyed. In seeking counsel the issue is obtaining help in clarifying one's thinking. At times, an individual may use godly counsel to help determine what is to be done. There is nothing unbiblical in this approach, as long as we recognize that: (1) in using this approach we do not shift the burden of responsibility from ourselves to the counselor—the individual is always accountable for his or her own decision; (2) using godly counsel as a fleece does not eliminate risk taking or the need to walk by faith.

Conclusion

Biblical application is a lifelong process. If any of us were able to completely assimilate and put the Scripture into practice, we would "arrive." Then application would cease to be a process and become a product. "Doing" is the outcome of "being." To the degree that we assimilate the ingredients that make up the process of Biblical application, we will "do" what is right. Meanwhile, we continue to wrestle with the issues God raises in our lives. That, after all, *is* the process.

Appendix

Bill, a man in his twenties, is a partner with his father. Together they run a large, successful insurance agency.

Bill's dad is a "self-made man." He started the company from scratch and is proud of his accomplishments. He is also proud of Bill and delighted that they are working together. Dad wants Bill to run the business, but he can't resist the temptation to step in and make unilateral decisions. When this happens, the employees become confused, and Bill becomes frustrated.

Since Bill is a Christian, he has wrestled before the Lord over how he should respond. In studying David's life, he found his answer. His application came from his study of 1 Samuel 24 and 26. It is both an illustration of what biblical application is all about and how to draw an application from an Old Testament example.

WAIT UPON THE LORD—1 SAMUEL 24 AND 26
A STUDY OF MY RELATIONSHIP WITH DAD
AND THE BUSINESS

1. David would not take matters into his own hands. He knew he was going to be king—but he also knew Saul was the Lord's anointed. It was up to God to remove him.

   Application: Dad is president by God's choice. I should do nothing directly to change that. I can make my feelings known, but I should not demand or push.

2. David was at peace knowing that his time to be king would come; sooner or later Saul would be removed by the Lord (1 Samuel 26:10).

Application: In God's time, I will have the leadership role in the company—or in some other area that God chooses.

3. David recognized that the Lord repays each man for his righteousness and his faithfulness (1 Samuel 26:23; Psalm 18:20). Therefore he knew that by refusing to kill Saul, he would be *positively* repaid by the Lord.

   Application: Not taking matters into my own hands (obedience and faithfulness) will be rewarded by the Lord.

4. David did not want to talk negatively about Saul or undermine him in any way. He even regretted cutting off the corner of Saul's robe (1 Samuel 24:4–6).

   Application: I should do nothing to undermine Dad's authority or influence. I should not put him down in any way. I have indirectly talked against him by letting employees know that I wanted to get certain things done before he returned.

5. David knew it would be a *sin* to take matters into his own hands prematurely (1 Samuel 26:9). He would be heavy with guilt.

   Application: It would be a sin for me to act prematurely— ahead of God.

6. It was because of his devotion to God, not because of his devotion to Saul, that David spared Saul (1 Samuel 24:6: "Far be it from me *because of the Lord* that I should do this thing").

   Application: Far be it from me to try to change Dad or take matters into my own hands, not just because he is my Dad but because of my devotion to God.

7. David's decision to spare Saul was not because of good behavior on Saul's part or because Saul deserved to be spared (1 Samuel 24:11, 27; 1 Samuel 26:21).

   Application: My reactions are not to be a response to Dad's behavior or what I think he deserves.

8. David let Saul know the limits of his options—that he would not try to unseat or move Saul aside but instead would wait upon God (1 Samuel 24:11; 26:11).

   Application: I need to let Dad know that he is *secure* in our company as president until he or God changes that.

9. Saul was convicted of his offense against David but then returned to his old ways of chasing David (1 Samuel 24:17; 26:2; I Samuel 26:21).

   Application: Don't expect Dad's behavior to change. He will probably still struggle with his ego and need to control at times. Also, he may be unwilling to have less ownership interest and will desire to keep money in the business.

10. David did not listen to the worldly advice of those around him (1 Samuel 24:4; 26:8).

    Application: The counselor who told me not to take responsibility for Dad's ego but to push forward, gave me wrong advice.

11. David had a young man killed who had killed Saul (or said he killed Saul at Saul's request), because he stretched out his hand to kill the Lord's anointed (2 Samuel 1:14–16).

    Application: I cannot allow others to undermine Dad's position.

12. David truly loved Saul and built him up even after his death (1 Samuel 1:19–27). He wrote a song about Saul and Jonathan.

Application: My entire relationship should be one of love for Dad, and I should build him up.

13. After Saul's death, David first asked the Lord how to proceed (2 Samuel 2:1). He was then satisfied to be king only over Judah for seven and a half years (2 Samuel 5:5). He was thirty when he became King of Judah.

Application: Don't rush ahead, even if you see a green light. Move slowly as God leads.

WHY COULD DAVID HAVE THIS ATTITUDE?

1. He recognized that the battle was the Lord's. He could rest in this assurance because of his experiences of God's faithfulness and a proper understanding of his limitations and God's position. 1 Samuel 17:47 says: "It is not by sword or spear that the LORD saves; for the battle is the LORD's, and he will give all of you into our hands."

2. He believed that God would deliver him, no matter what the circumstances (1 Samuel 17:37).

3. He received strength when he needed it from the Lord. 1 Samuel 30:6: "But David found strength himself in the Lord his God."

4. He had a pure heart. 1 Samuel 16:7: "The LORD looks at the heart."

5. The Holy Spirit's power worked through his life. 1 Samuel 16:13: "From that day on the Spirit of the LORD came upon David in power."

6. He remembered past times of deliverance by the Lord. 1 Samuel 17:37: "The LORD who delivered me from the paw of the lion and the paw of the bear will deliver me from the hand of this Philistine."

7. He was vocal that all battles were in God's name (strength), not his own. 1 Samuel 17:45: "I come against you in the name of the LORD Almighty, the God of the armies of Israel, whom you have defied."

8. He sought godly counsel. He spent time with Samuel and sought his counsel on how to handle the situation (1 Samuel 19:18).

9. He had the support of others—Jonathan and all Israel and Judah (1 Samuel 18:16; 20:4).

10. David truly loved Saul and Jonathan in spite of his treatment by Saul (1 Samuel 20:41, 42).